360

Motorbooks International

MUSCLE CAR COLOR HISTORY

CHEVROLET SMALL-BLOCK V-8

Anthony Young

First published in 1992 by Motorbooks International Publishers & Wholesalers, PO Box 2, 729 Prospect Avenue, Osceola, WI 54020 USA

Motorbooks International books are also available at discounts in bulk quantity for industrial or sales-promotional use. For details write to Special Sales Manager at the Publisher's address

Library of Congress Cataloging-in-Publication Data
Young, Anthony
Chevrolet small-block V-8 / Anthony Young. p.cm. — (Motorbooks International muscle car color history)
Includes index.
ISBN 0-87938-575-8
1. Chevrolet automobile—Motors—History.
I. Title. II. Series.
TL215.C5Y68 1992
629.25'04—dc20 91-33643

Printed and bound in Hong Kong

On the front cover: *The rare 1967 Camaro Z/28 had a special 302 ci small-block beneath the hood. It was officially rated at 290 hp, but actually produced more like 375 hp in basic showroom trim. Set up for Trans-Am racing, the Z/28 was good for some 450 hp. Only 602 Z/28 cars were built in 1967.* Mike Mueller

On the frontispiece: *The 327 ci small-block engine of the 1963 Corvette Z06.* Jerry Heasley

On the title page: *The new generation of Corvettes arrived in 1984 after an hiatus development year in 1983. For the first year of production, the 350ci small-block came with only the throttle-body fuel injection, but starting with this 1985 model, the tuned-port injection was available.*

On the back cover: *Small-blocks power these matched Corvettes through a turn in Corvette Challenge racing, photography by Mark Weber; the LT1 engine, which Chevrolet developed by re-engineering its 350 ci small-block V-8. It was introduced in the 1992 Corvette and given the legendary engine code.*

Contents

Acknowledgments

History is not something car companies are in the business of preserving. They are in the business of building cars. The cars and engines they used to build are often of little concern to them. Automobile companies prosper on the production of current models and the research, design and development of cars for future production.

Events as they happen are rarely looked upon as historic at the time. Hindsight, however, shows certain events *were* historic. This is particularly true of automobiles, and it is especially true of Chevrolet automobiles. However, it seems no one is around to record and preserve those events for the sake of future historians. The events are only significant years after the fact.

Chevrolet has produced some of the most significant cars and engines in automotive history. No doubt they were seen as important at the time, but they were never thought of as important to Chevrolet enthusiasts of the future. There are no archives at Chevrolet, per se, only the photographic books in Public Relations, where I got the bulk of the black and white photographs for this book.

While doing research for this book, I learned some horror stories that are truly amazing from an historic standpoint. For example, Terry Boyce, author of a number of Chevrolet books, told me that the original, full-size line drawings of the 1953 Corvette were eventually thrown away in the course of numerous moves. General Motors reorganized in the early eighties, which resulted in manufacturing, engineering, sales and design materials being scattered throughout the organization. A great deal of historic material was, inevitably, thrown away during this reorganization. On an individual level, the natural tendency when moving is to clean out the drawers so as not to have to haul all that "old stuff" to the new location. Memos, papers, drawings, even photographs, usually went into the "circular file."

Paul Prior is a name familiar to many Chevrolet enthusiasts, having worked for Chevrolet for thirty years, most of that time alongside Vince Piggins in Product Promotion. He has firsthand knowledge of how history repeats itself when it comes to preserving historic production cars.

"Once in a while, on a Corvette anniversary," Prior states, "they decide, 'Hey, we don't have one of these old ones,' so they'll conduct a big search and find the earliest serial number they can, buy the car, restore it—I mean put *tons* of money into restoring it—and then when this particular activity is over, they'll sell the thing again! They've done this two or three times.

"I suppose management thinks, 'Well, if we're going to save this stuff, *where* are we going to save it?' You have to create a budget to do it. Whose budget are we going to take this out of? Engineering says, 'Not ours.' The sales department would say, 'Not ours.' I think you get the picture."

No doubt there have been many at Chevrolet who would have liked to preserve Chevrolet product literature, photographs, drawings and other documents, and even examples of significant cars and engines, but the predicament is precisely as Prior stated.

Fortunately, Chevrolet has seen fit to preserve photographs of its cars and engines. Within Chevrolet Public Relations is a special room dedicated primarily to the storage of these photographs, as well as current product literature. The majority of these photographs—from the fifties to the eighties—are bound in heavy binders and have been preserved beautifully. There were also hanging files of photos both prior to the fifties and after the eighties.

I would like to thank Tom Hoxie for permission to spend several days reviewing these files, as well as Kari St. Antoine and Mark Broderick for answering my questions and supplying photographs.

Down the hall from Public Relations is The Raceshop—a far cry from the low-key efforts of Product Promotion in years past. Wes Yocum was most helpful to me as I researched the origins of the current 5.7 liter—350 cubic inches to Chevy enthusiasts—High Output V-8 engine assembly anyone can order over the Chevrolet parts counter. He directed me to Jim Covey, who explained to me at length how this superb engine came to be.

Jack Underwood, who is Powertrain Liaison for Product Information on V-8 engines, supplied me with a wealth of printed matter in the form of S.A.E. papers, internal corporate and division documents, and Chevrolet manuals.

Dorothy Dickerson of GM Powertrain Public Affairs supplied the photo of a rarely seen aspect of the small-block V-8—its assembly. Fans of the L98 will find this photo in the chapter covering the nineties.

Brian Czarnowczan, in GM's Service Technology Group, provided the exploded view and part description of the L98 that appears in the appendix.

Those high-performance parts and engines are described in the General Motors Performance Parts Catalog—a smorgasbord of Chevrolet, Buick, Pontiac and Oldsmobile performance parts. This slick catalog was put together by High Performance Communications of Santa Cruz, California. I would like to thank Rick Voeglin at HPC for the photograph of the 5.7 liter H.O. V-8.

Without question it is the personal recollections of the engineers who spoke with me that make this history of the small-block so interesting. I would like to thank Bill Howell, Maurice Rosenberger, Paul Prior, Dick Keinath, Fred Frincke, Don McPherson, Fred Sherman, Dave Martens, Joe Bertsch, Louis Cuttitta, Jim Walker, and Bob Wiltse.

An authority on Chevrolet history is Pat Chappell. She was the first to steer me in the right direction, with sources to contact. It was her book, *Standard Catalog of Chevrolet 1912-1990,* that I used to get the horsepower and torque levels for the small-block over the years. I would highly recommend this exhaustively researched and expertly written book to every Chevrolet enthusiast.

Finally, I would like to thank my wife, Annie, for her encouragement and sacrifice so I could write this book, which is dedicated to small-block fans everywhere.

The 1989 Corvette was available with style and power. Chevrolet brought back the convertible hardtop after a decade's absence, and the car was available with the 245 hp L98 engine. Thus equipped, the car posted a 0-60 mph time of 5.8 seconds and covered the quarter-mile in 14.4 seconds at 94 mph. Chevrolet

16
16

Introduction

Swiss-born Louis Chevrolet started building the cars that carried his name in 1912 under the direction of William C. Durant, founder of General Motors. Durant lost control of GM in 1910 to the banks holding the purse strings. The Chevrolet was part of Durant's plan to regain control of General Motors, which he did in September 1915. By that time, however, Louis Chevrolet had had serious disagreements with Durant over what a Chevrolet should be, and the young racer/engineer had departed. Durant retained the rights to the Chevrolet name and continued to use it.

Until 1917, the only engines offered in Chevrolets were in-line four- and six-cylinder designs. However, late in 1917, production began of the company's first V-8, which would be installed in the D-4 four-passenger roadster and the D-5 five-passenger touring model.

The engine featured a cast-iron block with a bore of 3.375 in. and a stroke of 4.00 in. It had a displacement of 288 ci. With a Zenith double-jet carburetor, it developed thirty-six net horsepower, about fifteen more than the in-line four-cylinder engine offered in the 490 series and FA series models for 1918.

In California in 1957, poor little rich boy Lance Reventlow decided to build his own sports racer to challenge the Ferraris, Jaguars and Corvettes. He called his creation the Scarab, and the first type of sports racer, left, featured a Chevrolet small-block V-8 mounted in the front. Initially the small-block was run at the stock 283 ci, but within a short time the engines were up to 339 ci with a bore and stroke job. The Scarab ruled the US road race world for several years before Reventlow went on to create his Formula 1 car, right, to take on Europe. It was as dismal a failure as the sports racer had been a success. David Gooley

During most of the "Roaring Twenties," in-line four-cylinder engines powered Chevrolets exclusively, in an effort to keep the car as competitive with Ford as possible. In 1929, that changed. The four-cylinder engines were dropped completely, and now only in-line six-cylinder engines would power General Motors' value leader.

The fifties saw many changes in automobiles, and the biggest was widespread introduction of the V-8. Chevrolet was among the last to do so, but when its V-8 did appear, it succeeded in capturing the interest of millions of car buyers. The Saturday-night racers saw an affordable powerplant that was supremely easy to work on and to hot-rod to get more power. With the small-block's inherent design integrity, Chevrolet was able to keep up with the demands for more power without having to alter the engine block's basic dimensions.

In 1958, Chevrolet introduced a new V-8 engine with a displacement of 348 ci. The engine block and cylinder head were completely different from that of the smaller-displacement V-8. The terms "small-block" and "big-block" were coined to differentiate the two engines, and these descriptive words have stuck ever since.

Despite the many improvements to the small-block over the decades, it should be pointed out here just how little the bare block has changed in terms of overall dimensions. Putting a 305-ci or 350-ci block next to the first 265-ci block would be revealing. The cylinder bore centers have remained at 4.40 inches. The 265-ci V-8 block had an overall length of 21.75 in.; the current 305-ci block has an overall length of 20.19 in. and the 350-ci block is slightly shorter at 19.93 in. But here's the most interesting fact: the 265-ci block weighed 147 pounds; the current 350-ci block weighs 151.5 pounds—a difference of less than five pounds!

This book was not only written for the countless numbers of Chevrolet small-block enthusiasts. As I was researching this book, I also became aware of a new generation of engineers at Chevrolet involved with the small-block today who don't know the engine's roots or how it evolved over the years. These men and women are following in the steps of engineers whose names are only vaguely familiar to them, if at all. This fact hit home when I spoke with one young man in the engineering library who had never heard of Vince Piggins.

In this book you will learn how the small-block V-8 was conceived, designed, tested and built, often from those who were involved with the engine themselves over the years. The emphasis here has been on passenger car use; the subject of the small-block's racing heritage has been dealt with at length in other books and magazine articles. It is my hope this book does justice to the most successful and long-lived V-8 engine ever bolted into an automobile.

Anthony Young
July 1991

The air cleaner setup for the 1956 265 ci Dual Quad small-block was a massive affair with dual air filters hung from both sides of the t-shaped air intake. The Dual Quad engine knocked almost a full second off the 0-60 mph acceleration time over the 265 ci V-8. Jerry Heasley

The 1956 265 ci Dual Quad small-block with its air cleaner system removed, showing the open barrels of the carburetors. By 1957, the two four-barrels produced 245 hp at 5000 rpm with hydraulic valve lifters or 270 hp at 6000 rpm with solid lifters. Compression in either case was set at 9.5:1. Jerry Heasley

Previous page
The first Chevrolet to receive the new small-block V-8 was the 1955 line. By 1956, the Corvette Dual Quad 265 ci small-block was available in the Bel Air line and it upped the ante on Chevrolet performance. Jerry Heasley

matic transmission that Oldsmobile used in 1937 and Buick used it in 1938. During that time we developed what became the Hydramatic that Oldsmobile started to use in 1940. Cadillac put it in in 1941. Then the war came and they shut down automaking in February of 1942."

During the war years, Rosenberger worked on a program to adapt two Cadillac V-8 engines to a special transfer case transmission to power light tanks contracted by the War Department. As quickly as Cadillac automobile production had stopped in 1942, it started, with the end of the war, for the 1946 model year. He continued to work for Cadillac for the next six years. Rosenberger had distinguished himself at Cadillac, and this hadn't gone unnoticed by Ed Cole. In 1952, Rosenberger moved to Chevrolet and started work in the experimental department. There, he worked on isolating the troublesome noises the 265 V-8 generated in the prototype cars, as well as on general car development.

"Cole started board work on the small-block V-8 engine in the summer and fall of 1952," Rosenberger remembered. "I think he decided he would abandon the engine that Ed Kelly and other Chevrolet engineers had designed. He got 'hold of experienced GM engine people he knew—and he knew many—and got their input."

The drafting room at Chevrolet became a hotbed of activity after Cole arrived. Dave Martens was there when it all began.

"I started as a college graduate student-in-training in January 1952," said Martens. "For the next two years I was alternately a draftsman and worked in the various plants and laboratories, then I was a draftsman full time.

"At the time Ed Cole and Harry Barr came to Chevrolet from Cadillac, Chevrolet had, as I remember, a 231-cubic inch V-8 engine on the boards, and they even built a couple. When Cole came in, they scrapped that design and started over, more or less on the basis of how the

With two four-barrel carburetors and dual exhausts, the 1956 Dual Quad 265 ci Bel Air was a muscle car before its time. Production of the Dual Quad cars was limited. Jerry Heasley

Cadillac 331-cubic inch V-8 was done, which he had worked on.

"Al Kolbe was the assistant staff engineer in charge of the design of the 265-cubic inch V-8. He was low-key—a pure designer—and would spend most of his time in the drafting room, sitting down at the drafting boards with the designer, suggesting this, suggesting that, sketching what he wanted. The configuration of the 265 V-8, I would have to say, was basically [made up of] his ideas. Yes, Ed Cole was responsible for ramrodding the program through, but Al Kolbe did the actual design work. He did not want to get any notoriety. He wasn't interested in writing an S.A.E. paper or any of that—he was a pure designer. Al Kolbe was, in my opinion, not properly recognized for the design genius that he was," Martens said, emphatically.

"Kolbe would be in the drafting room every day," Martens continued. "Cole would visit the drafting room once a week because his activities were running a lot more at Chevrolet than just the new engine design."

As chief of passenger-car chassis design for Chevrolet Motor Division, Russell F. Sanders worked closely with the engine design engineers from the very beginning. He received his bachelor of science degree in mechanical engineering from Michigan State College in 1929. After graduating, he joined the Oldsmobile Division of General Motors. In 1934 he was assigned to the Chevrolet Motor Division. When it came time for Chevrolet to begin its work on a V-8 engine, Sanders met continually with the engine team to ensure engine-to-chassis compatibility. He wrote a paper for the Society of Automotive Engineers chronicling the development work on the Chevrolet V-8, and, from the outset, this engine was conceived and designed with different goals in mind.

Not the least of the discussions centered around displacement. This was basic, because it established bore, stroke and overall block dimensions.

"In our research over a period of years," Sanders wrote, "we have investigated many types of V-8 engine. During the early stages, we developed an engine with 231 cubic inches of displacement, but with changing conditions, a greater displacement was considered desirable. At one of our group meetings we sketched some basic outlines to indicate just what we wanted in height, displacement, length and so forth. We began thinking about a 245 cubic inch engine, but when we got further into this study we found we could just as well go to

The 265 ci V-8 was a marvel of simplicity and economy. It wasn't long, however, before enthusiasts saw the performance potential of the new V-8. Chevrolet kept up with the demand, pushing output far beyond one horsepower per cubic inch in just a few years.

about 260 or 265 with no penalty of extra weight, knowing that ample displacement is fundamentally the most economical way to insure high torque and resultant good performance economy."

After much discussion, a bore size of 3.75 inches was selected. To achieve a 260-ci displacement, a 2.93 in. stroke was required. The engineers decided to round this off to 3.00 inches, which resulted in a 265-ci displacement for the engine. Cylinder bore centers were fixed at 4.40 inches. With this information, the length of the crankshaft was determined. After factoring in the width for main bearings, connecting rod bearing, crankshaft arms and engine block bulkheads, the overall length of the engine block was 21.75 inches.

Chevrolet engineers felt it was unnecessary to carry the block more than .125 in. below the centerline of the crankshaft. This was just enough, in their view, for solid placement of the main bearing caps in a machined notch and was in line with their goal of keeping weight down.

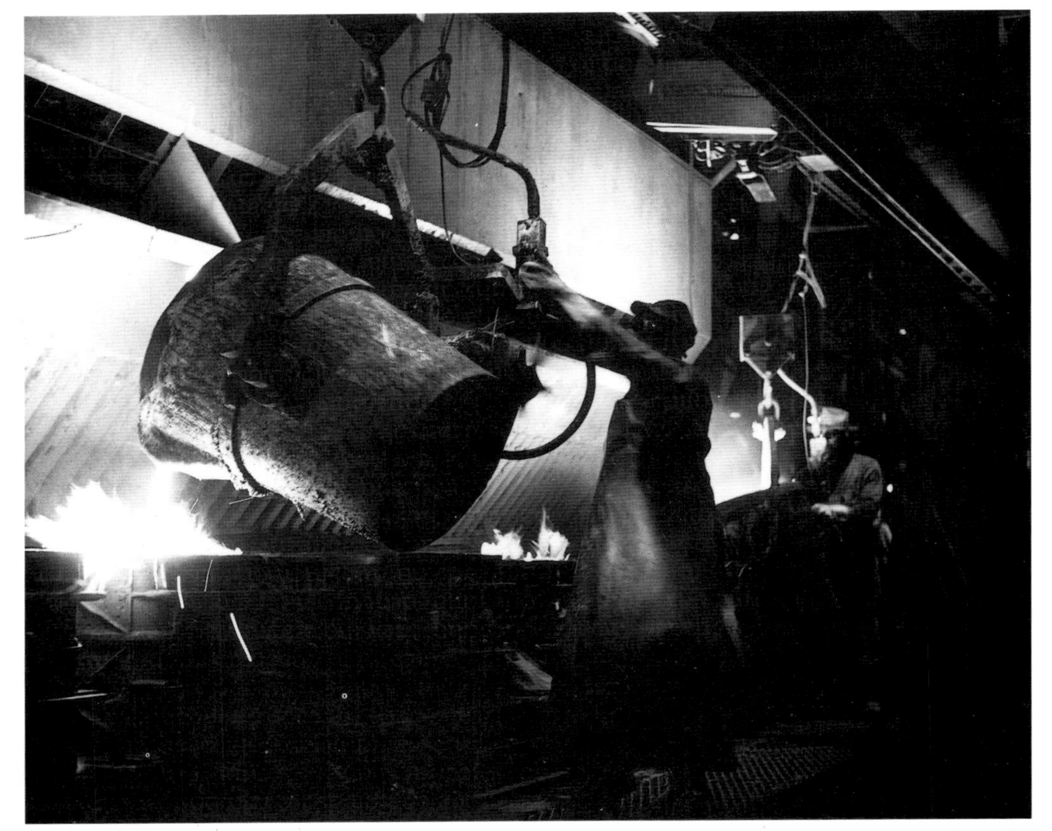

This shot shows the molten iron being poured into drag molds with the engine block sand cores. This was definitely one of the hottest jobs in the foundry! After proper cooling, the sand cores were broken and removed and the raw castings sent to the machining line.

Chevrolet refined its V-8 casting procedures with its prototypes. The 265-ci V-8 block was meant to be a precision casting. By reducing the number of cores, it reduced the tolerance error resulting from core stackup variations.

"Fewer cores," Sanders wrote, "mean that our section thicknesses can be controlled much more accurately, and we have less sand to handle. The end result is a precision casting which is lighter, as well as lower in cost."

There were nine major and three minor cores to cast the 265-ci V-8 block. Another manufacturer required twenty-two cores to cast its V-8. Chevrolet reduced the number of cores required by mating the left and right-hand cylinder-barrel cores in a "V" with an integral crank chamber core. These four cores were put on a slab. Two, one-piece jacket cores were slipped over each bank of cylinder cores. The jacket cores were supported in position and prevented from moving by the end cores of the block. These end cores, also mounted on the slab, formed the contours of the timing chain case and front structure, and at the rear, the clutch housing attachment configuration.

The entire assembly of cores was placed in a drying fixture. After drying, it was moved to the casting line, known as a drag mold. Any loose sand was blown out and pouring of molten iron was performed in a smooth operation. After cooling, the cores were removed and broken, and loose sand dislodged. The casting then moved on to the machining phase. The fully-machined 265-ci V-8 block weighed only 147 pounds, compared to 163 pounds for Chevrolet's in-line six-cylinder block.

The Cylinder Head

With an eye toward cost and proven performance characteristics, Chevrolet chose the wedge-type combustion chamber with in-line valves for its cylinder head.

"We settled on the high-turbulence, wedge-type design for combustion control and combustion smoothness," Sanders wrote, "since it controls the rate of pressure rise in the chamber. We feel that the type of chamber which exposes a high volume of the charge early in the burn cycle and then goes out into a quench area gives low octane requirement and smoothness of operation."

The designer of the cylinder head for the 265-ci V-8 was Don McPherson. "Cole came in one day," he remembered, "and said, 'I want the smallest, lightest-weight cylinder head you can come up with.' This was back when I was design supervisor, but they put me back on the board to do that head, about 1953. I made sketches of the cross-section of the head—a whole bunch of them—and the smaller I made them, the better Cole liked them. Finally, I had a cross-section of the head where we just barely had room for the rocker arms and the rocker arm cover, and he bought it.

"On the cylinder head itself, a big problem there was squeezing in enough water, by our standards, around the valve guides. We ended up, actually, with less water around the valve guides than any engine at the time, and that was more a tribute to what the foundry people were able to do, I think, than what we were able to draw. That was a real, real tight job.

"The biggest problem with the cylinder head," McPherson continued, "was that Cole wanted it very small, and he didn't want any excess machining on there. He wanted a cast surface on the top for the [valve cover] gasketing sur-

Finished bare blocks were sent through this Sheffield air gauge to check each cylinder bore, with the results reflected on the machine directly in front of the operator. The blocks then proceeded to the engine assembly phase.

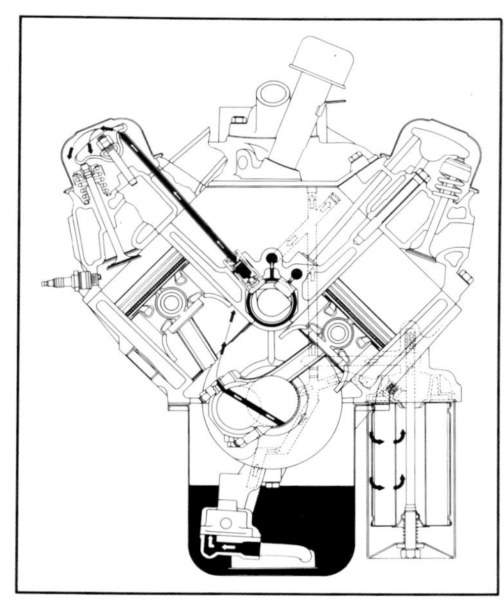

This cross-section of the 265 V-8 clearly shows the oiling system developed for the small-block. The hydraulic lifters actually pumped the oil up through the pushrods, past a hole in the rocker arm and over the valvetrain components. The stamped steel "umbrella" over the valve spring helped eliminate oil burning.

The new Chevrolet Engineering Center, shown in the center of this photo, offered vastly improved facilities for the research, design and engineering of new engines and vehicles. The front portion of the building held the engineering offices. Clearly visible along the entire south side of the building are the engine dynamometer test cells. Behind the dyno cells are the machine shops and garages.

Interior of the 1958 Corvette was all-American 1950s glitz with flowing curves and acres of chrome. The flashy styling has never been bettered. Musclecar Review

face. That was the first time that had ever been done. Except for the spring seats, there was no machined surface on the top because the bosses for the rocker arm studs were higher than the basic surface for the rocker cover, so there was no way, without getting a traversing mill that went around there, to do that thing properly. We ended up with just a cast surface there, and then we had to develop gaskets for that doggone thing, and we never did a particularly good job of it.

"Another problem we had with the cylinder head," McPherson added, "was how do you get the oil back down into the crankcase? We designed a trough at the back end that would drain down through the block, but the blow-by of the engine was so high that the blow-by would keep the oil from coming back down the engine. This was a very severe problem. What we ended up doing was casting some chambers in the back of the cylinder head, then drilled holes down through the cylinder head into the crankcase so we didn't have all that blow-by pushing oil back up. That was a last-minute change that we rushed into production."

Each cylinder head used a total of seventeen bolts to secure the head to the block. A five-bolt pentagon pattern was used around each combustion chamber, instead of the usual four bolts.

When all the sand cores of each cylinder head were assembled, the fixture was inverted before being put into the drag mold. The cylinder head was cast in this manner to get harder iron at the "bottom" of the head, around the valve seats. The combustion chamber was cast to shape; the only machining necessary in the chamber was for the valve seats.

Rocker covers are not often an aesthetic concern, but on Chevrolet's new V-8, Cole felt they should be special, within cost parameters. It's a funny story, one which McPherson retold.

"Cole came in one day and said, 'I want a sexy rocker cover'," McPherson laughed. It should be stated here that McPherson was noted at Chevrolet for his dry sense of humor, and could be relied upon to respond with a perfectly straight face that would leave other engineers aghast. He answered Cole by suggesting the ends of the rocker covers resemble the upper frontal superstructure of the female anatomy. Cole was not amused.

The Corvette came alive as Chevrolet's sports car with the addition of the new small-block V-8 in 1955. By 1958, this Corvette coupe was available with a 283 ci small-block in either carbureted or fuel-injection form. The charcoal and black two-toning in the fender coves was an extra-cost option. Musclecar Review

The exhaust manifolds were located near the top of the cylinder head, with the manifold going up, over, then down in the center, a pattern with which Chevrolet enthusiasts of the fifties are familiar. This made for very short exhaust passages in the cylinder head; these passages had water jackets above and below.

Intake Manifold

Chevrolet engineers studied the intake manifold to combine a number of functions and try to "clean up" the appearance of the top of the engine. Besides its fuel intake function, the Chevrolet intake manifold included: a provision for hot water heater take-off; a cross-over for exhaust-heat to the two-barrel carburetor; a distributor mounting; an oil filler; a thermostat housing; a water outlet to the radiator; and a water temperature gauge hole.

The intake manifold was designed in such a way as to seal to the top of the engine, eliminating the need for a separate tappet-chamber cover. Instead of openings between the intake passages, as was typical with other makes, there were webs. This one-piece design also eliminated complex parting lines during casting, with their resulting "flash" requiring additional machining.

Reciprocating Parts

For its V-8, Chevrolet studied both the alloy-iron, or cast, crankshaft and the forged crankshaft. Forged steel was selected because of a high modulus, or degree, of elasticity and specific gravity. Chevrolet could also employ its vast forging capacity at its facilities. New forging processes were used to reduce draft angles and make the crankshaft as short as possible.

"Our crankshaft design made it possible to produce what we believe to be the smallest and lightest commercial V-8 power package for its displacement," Sanders boasted.

The flat-top piston was aluminum with a piston pin offset of 5/64 in. toward the major thrust face to avoid piston slap and give ample tolerances on piston fit for manufacturing economy. The piston

The fuel-injected 283 ci 1958 Corvette engine was available as either RPO 579, which produced 250 hp, or RPO 579D, which produced 290 hp. The difference in performance was largely based on the grind of the cam. Either fuel-injected engine cost $484.20 versus the $182.95 of the top carbureted, 270 hp small-block—more than double the price for only an ounce more horsepower. Musclecar Review

The 283 ci V-8 was introduced in 1957. It used a larger 3.876 in. bore, but retained the 3.00 in. stroke of the 265 ci V-8. The 283 became a perennial favorite with millions of Chevrolet enthusiasts. This is the 220 hp version with single four-barrel carburetor. Note the different exhaust manifolds from those on the 265 ci V-8.

was a three-ring design. Chevrolet spent a considerable amount of time examining the oil consumption problem under high vacuum conditions such as deceleration. They found oil passed the piston rings not between the ring and the cylinder wall, but between the ring and the piston ring groove. Chevrolet solved this problem, after numerous different designs, with a new type of expander between two oil control rings in that piston ring groove.

The connecting rod had a 5.70-in. center-to-center distance. The piston pin was pressed into the connecting rod during assembly. The connecting rod underwent eighteen million cycles in testing rather than the usual ten million with 2,400-lb tension and 7,000-lb compression without a failure.

Valvetrain

Rather than go with rocker arms mounted on a single rocker shaft, Chevrolet took a different approach. The designer of the Chevrolet swivel-ball rocker arm system was Clayton Leach, who later became assistant chief engineer of Pontiac. Each rocker arm was a precision stamping which pivoted on a stud pressed into the cylinder head.

The rocker arms were made from 1010 steel, carbonitrided and hardened to a depth of from 0.010 to 0.020 in., the surface treated. Once assembled over the valve stem and pushrod, the rocker arm was retained on the stud with a fulcrum ball and locknut.

This made it supremely easy to adjust each valve for lash, regardless of whether the lifters (tappets) were hydraulic, as was the case here, or mechanical, which came on V-8s with manual transmissions.

Proper oiling of the valvetrain was something Cole wanted to ensure, particularly with the use of the stamped steel rocker arms.

"The big development on that thing was how to get oil up to the rocker arm," McPherson said. "The fellow who worked on that was Bob Papenguth. He did the work on the wafer in the tappet that metered the oil up the pushrod to the rocker arm. That was the key to the success of the thing. In the past, they had always had complicated systems that got the oil topside and down through the center shaft on the rocker arms. But this thing took the oil up through the tappet and the pushrod and around the ball.

Without that development, it would have been an impossibility."

Research and Development

Work on the 265-ci V-8 proceeded quickly, and by the spring of 1953, prototypes were running in Chevrolet's engineering lab on Holbrook Avenue in Hamtramck. Dick Keinath was right in the middle of his two-year training program when he became involved with the 265-ci V-8's valvetrain testing. Keinath performed the first deflection studies on the rocker arms.

"We were doing deflection work to see how strong the studs, stud attachments, the rocker arms and the pushrods were," he remembered. Keinath was yet another new engineer in the right place at the right time at Chevrolet, which permitted him to become involved in one of the most exciting engineering programs in the company's history. Because he was fortunate enough to be involved with Chevrolet's new V-8, he eventually went on to become assistant staff engineer, then chief engineer of engines years later.

But in 1950, Keinath was a graduate of Michigan State University with a bachelor's degree in mechanical engineering. Like many others who applied to General Motors, he had worked on and had rebuilt automobile engines as a teenager. That year, he began working in General Motors Product Study in the area of automatic transmissions. These included the Buick Dynaflow and Chevrolet's Power Glide. Keinath's mentor was none other than Maurice Rosenberger.

In 1952, Keinath transferred from GM's Engineering Staff to Chevrolet and began that division's very extensive training program. The program exposed the engineer to all phases of automotive design engineering, manufacturing and testing.

"When I transferred to Chevrolet," he explained, "I joined the training program. The training period included a three-month assignment at the design center, a three-month assignment in the laboratory, where I did work on the small-block, a three-month assignment at the GM Proving Grounds, three months at the engine plant in Flint, Michigan, a period of time at the grey iron foundry in Saginaw, Michigan, another couple of months at the manual transmission plant in Saginaw, another three months at the automatic transmission plant in Cleveland, Ohio, some time at the Tonawanda, New York, engine plant, some time at the gear and axle plant in Detroit, also three months at the metallurgical laboratory in Detroit. Then it included another period of time actually in the V-8 engine design group in Detroit across the street from the GM building in what we lovingly referred to as 'The Bank Building.'

"In 1954, management took the engine design group and the transmission design group and removed them from the main General Motors building and rented this old bank building across the street which was about 100 years old. They had old tapestries on the walls, a ceiling about 40 feet high, columns in front—an old, old building. It was dirty, drafty, the most unlikely building to use as a design center, because everyone had to have their own fluorescent lamp to get light on their own board. The bathrooms didn't work, and when there was a heavy rain, the basement flooded. When the front door opened, the breeze would come in and blow dirt, dust and everything all over the boards. Anything you happened to have on the boards would fly away."

When Fred Sherman joined Chevrolet in April 1954, developmental testing of the 265 V-8 was well underway.

"I started in the dynamometer cells. The V-8 was underway as far as development, almost a preproduction version of what was going to be released in the 1955 Chevrolet. The engines were measured on the dynamometer with open exhaust, which were tubes that were twelve feet long and about 2.5 in. in diameter, spark-adjusted and mixture-adjusted for maximum torque, corrected for 60 degrees Fahrenheit. Fan horsepower was added to that and that produced a figure that was at that time called advertised [gross] horsepower."

The facilities with which Sherman and his fellow technicians had to work were, indeed, antiquated. Ground had been broken for a new Chevrolet Engineering Center in Warren, Michigan, north of Twelve Mile Road, but it would be two years before the complex would be open. Sherman remembered what the old dyno facilities were like.

"We were at Holbrook and St. Aubin, which is now part of the gear and axle complex. At the old complex we had exposed control panels with all the contacts for the rheostats. The dynamometers there could no longer handle the output of the engines we were testing. At one point during the testing of a Corvette engine, the dynamometer actually overheated and began throwing flame out the back! They were fine for the straight sixes, and I imagine that lab had been there when they still had four-cylinder Chevrolets."

During 1954, many 265-ci V-8-equipped Chevrolets were driven extensively to expose any engine or vehicle problems. There were numerous vexing problems that had to be worked out, problems that Ed Cole and Harry Barr would not tolerate.

"Cole was organizing trips," Rosenberger remembered, "and would go on trips with us, for a day or two. I remember going down through Ohio one day in 1954, I think it was. We had a bunch of cars and started on a trip. We got out a ways and many of them were smoking so bad, he said, 'Let's turn around and fix this damn thing.' The smoking was due to ring design, and some oil coming down the valve stems. We went back and probably put in a month or two of work and took another trip."

Sherman remembered not only the oil burning problem the engines were experienceing, but Cole's active participation in solving it.

"At the old lab, I remember Ed Cole coming in one time when we had this engine oiling problem. He came in there while we were working on one of the engines. He had his suit coat off, his sleeves rolled up and he was working right on the engine with us. Of course, we all called him Mr. Cole, which he didn't like, and he would say, 'Just call me Ed.' We did, but we were just a little hesitant about it. Finally, we did come up with a fix for the oil burning in that we put a sheet metal umbrella over the valve spring to shield the oil splash from going down the intake valve and the valve guide."

Oil burning wasn't the only problem. Whenever a new engine is installed in a new car, it creates a host of new operating parameters that can tax the patience of any engineer. Maurice Rosenberger experienced this challenge all too clearly.

"The engine and body mounts in the car and the silencing of the powerplant took a tremendous amount of work," he recalled, "because all the attached acces sories had a proclivity for vibratin some speed that's resonant with thing in the car. You have booms and buzzes and things that drive you nuts.

"A guy like Cole, *coming from Cadillac,*" Rosenberger emphasized, "wasn't putting up with that stuff at Chevrolet. We worked our tails off on things the average guy building the lowest car on the rung of the ladder probably wouldn't have worried about. I can remember we were working weekends and nights on things that annoyed us. You'd drive up a seven percent hill and if you happened to drive a certain speed, it would boom so bad it would drive you nuts. We had dozens of things like that to work on. I think it helped our reputation to put out a slick car right from the start compared to what we would have done if we hadn't had a guy like Cole around."

Yet another problem involved the rocker arm studs, and it was Alex Mair himself who learned about it—while street racing!

"When the first production models came out," Sherman recalled vividly, "cars with standard transmissions did not get hydraulic valve lifters, they were solid lifters."

He took one of the cars out on Northwestern Highway. In this area, Woodward Avenue and Northwestern Highway, was where they would run the so-called "Teenage Grand Prix" up and down the road. During one of these drag demonstrations, he pulled about six of the studs out of the cylinder heads, and the engine shut down.

"If you had a maximum diameter hole and a minimum diameter stud,"

The Corvette's small-block made it a natural for the burgeoning road-racing enthusiasm that was sweeping the United States in the 1950s. Here was an American sports car priced at a base of $3,591 that had much more power than the early British sports cars it could grid against. But while the small-block V-8 was state-of-the-art, the Corvette's handling was definitely behind the times. Chevrolet

Sherman explained "they could pull out. There were a number of proposals, one of which was simply thread them right into the head. But they didn't want to spend that kind of money with an engine like this."

The solution was to increase the stud's boss length and diameter to improve grip length and reduce hoop stress. A 9,000 lb. minimum-press load was added to the assembly specifications.

All the work that had gone into the Chevrolet 265 V-8 was about to reach fruition. The combined efforts of the engineers, designers, drafters and dyno lab technicians had, indeed, produced one of the finest and most affordable V-8s to ever come out of General Motors.

Comparative Specifications

Chevrolet's relentless efforts to cut weight from the engine paid off handsomely. Here's the breakdown comparing the new V-8 to the 235.5-ci in-line six-cylinder engine, in pounds:

	V-8	I-Six
Block	147	163
Cylinder Heads (per engine)	77	72
Crankshaft	47	79
Connecting Rods, Pistons & Rings	21	22
Intake Manifold	34	13
Exhaust Manifolds	17	16
Valvetrain	18	25
Total	531	572

By the 1990s, many original Corvette race cars from the 1950s were back in action on the vintage race circuit—including some street cars that have since been modified. Chevrolet

Zora Arkus-Duntov was the godfather of the Corvette and believed that winning races was essential to building the image of his sports car. The Corvette SR-2 was Arkus-Duntov's way of advertising the Corvette's potential, now boasting 1 hp per cubic inch of displacement in fuel-injected form. The SR-2 was basically a standard RPO racing Corvette clothed by an aerodynamic body that recalled the racing Jaguar D-Type. Chevrolet

The two-barrel version of the 265-ci V-8 developed 162 gross hp at 4400 rpm and 257 lb-ft of gross torque at 2200 rpm. The optional four-barrel version with dual exhaust developed 180 hp at 4600 rpm and 260 lb-ft of torque at 2800 rpm.

"New Look! New Life! New Everything!"

To herald the new V-8, Chevrolet made sure it went into a completely new car. The car was a product of GM styling chief Harley Earl and studio head Clare MacKichan. The 1955 Chevrolet looked so fresh and different from the 1954 model, the combination of styling with new V-8 power moved *Motor Trend* to say it was practically "a completely new *make* of car."

The factory sales brochure said as much: "New Look! New Life (V8 or 6)! New Everything!" The brochure went on to tout the V-8's virtues:

"Here's the valve-in-head V-8 as only the valve-in-head leader can build it. And here are some of the wonderful things it brings you: 162 horsepower with an 8-to-1 ultra-high compression ratio! Highly efficient oversquare design, which means less piston travel . . . less friction wear! Exceptionally high horsepower per pound! The great new Chevrolet V-8 delivers brilliant performance, surprisingly high gas mileage, and extra long life."

Chevrolet, indeed, had a sleeper on its hands. The 180-hp Power Pack with dual exhaust only added $59.00 to the price tag, so *Road & Track* decided to test one. The car was a two-door model 210 with 4-speed manual column shift and 4.11:1 rear axle ratio. It reached 60 mph in a respectable 9.7 seconds and covered the quarter-mile in 17.4 seconds.

Racers—both amateur and professional—came out of the woodwork to compete with the new Chevrolet V-8. The car did extremely well for itself in class and various trials. By June 1955, a Chevrolet ad appeared in magazines boasting, "Don't argue with this baby!" The ad went on to recount the class wins by the 180-hp "Super Turbo-Fire V-8" at Daytona Beach (where they still raced on the beach) and other NASCAR events.

However, the zenith of hyperbole was the ad that appeared in the September 1955 *Motor Trend*. No one would accuse Chevrolet of not beating its own drum:

"Who's running number ONE in competition where 'claims' don't count? Chevrolet, that's who! In NASCAR Short Track Division events, this '55 Chevrolet has brought home more winning points than any car in any price class. Engine and performance *claims* don't count in this league. Here you've either got it or you haven't!

"*Chevrolet's* got it! Enough high-powered punch to run the pants off the competition—*all competition*, including

Chevrolet's styling master was Bill Mitchell, who was also a race fan. Using the mule chassis from Arkus-Duntov's SS program, Mitchell built his own Sting Ray racer highlighted by its sleek bodywork that would eventually form the basis of the 1963 Sting Ray production car design. Mitchell's racer was based on a 283 ci small-block. Chevrolet

"At that time, we didn't have computers, so as we were doing the tests, he was compiling the horsepower and plotting it on a curve sheet. We had to go many rpms over the horsepower peak. I got up to 6400 rpm and I asked him, 'What do we look like?' He said, 'You won't believe what I'm going to tell you. Shut her down.' So I throttled it back. He said, 'Look at that.' And I said, 'Are you sure you calculated this right?' He said, 'Trust me.' We got over one horsepower per cubic inch. That engine was removed from the stand, drained and it was shipped off to a car race. I believe it went down to Daytona."

For 1958, Chevrolet introduced the 348-ci Turbo-Thrust V-8. This new engine was radically different from its small-block brethren. The 348-ci block was 1.50 in. longer, 2.60 in. wider and weighed over 100 lb. more than the 283 block. The 348-ci V-8 was not a bored and stroked version of the 283; it was a completely new design, and thus, not a member of the small-block family. It made sense, however, to add this larger engine to the lineup because market demands necessitated this move. Without it, Chevrolet would have been at a distinct disadvantage with buyers looking for something bigger than the 283 V-8.

Chevrolet made some fundamental changes to the 283 V-8 block for 1958. While the bore centers remained the same, the cylinder walls were made thicker; this would pay off later when displacement increases were achieved with larger bores. In addition, the engine mount bosses were moved from the front of the block to the sides.

The 348 V-8 restricted the variations of the 283 V-8. There were only three versions available for 1958: the 185-hp Turbo-Fire V-8 with 2-bbl carburetor and 8.5:1 compression ratio; the 230-hp Super Turbo-Fire V-8 with 4-bbl carburetor and 9.5:1 compression ratio; and the 250-hp Ramjet Fuel Injection V-8, also with a 9.5:1 compression ratio. The highly-touted 283-hp 283 V-8 was dropped.

While it had been a contender in stock car racing in the beginning, the small-block Chevy was soon left behind in the push for bigger and bigger displacement engines to power the stockers. Instead, the engine would become the premier street engine for millions of performance enthusiasts who either modified them for greater performance or just left them stock and cruised the streets of America from coast to coast. It was a simple engine to work on and easy to modify.

For 1959, the small-block engine lineup remained unchanged. Ramjet Fuel Injection was still available. *Road & Track* never missed a chance to test a new Corvette, and they did so again for 1959. The top-of-the-line Ramjet fuel-injection sat atop the 283 V-8, with its 10.5:1 compression ratio. Brake horsepower was 290 at 6200 rpm. Equipped with a four-speed manual transmission and a 4.11 rear axle, the test car reached 60 mph in 6.6 seconds, covering the quarter-mile in 14.5 seconds at 96 mph with a top speed of 128 mph.

The competitive image of the small-block was to receive a boost from an unexpected quarter. The NHRA (National Hot Rod Association) Nationals that year were held at Detroit Dragway on Labor Day weekend. Numerous Motor City executives were present, including Edward N. Cole. A 1957 Chevrolet took top eliminator title in the Super Stock class, proving the small-block could indeed hold its own on the dragstrip. It was a scene that would be repeated many times in different NHRA and AHRA (American Hot Rod Association) classes over the following decades.

As the fifties drew to a close, the trend in passenger car engines for the foreseeable future appeared to be one of continued displacement increases. Chevrolet would follow this trend, but the division wisely decided it would not abandon the basic qualities that made the small-block so practical, economical, durable—and popular.

The Sixties:
The Performance Decade

"We spent an awful lot of our time on performance development. That was a large part of the sales pitch that Cole wanted when he was General Manager."
Don McPherson

As the sixties dawned, the Chevrolet small-block had a bright future ahead. It would prove to be the most exciting era for enthusiasts because this was to be the performance decade and the spectre of government regulation and power-robbing emissions control wouldn't emerge in full force until the seventies.

During the sixties, Chevrolet introduced some of the finest examples of small-block engineering in the engine's history. There was the 327, introduced in 1962, and five years later, the high-revving 302 of Z-28 fame came out. Perhaps the greatest of all the small-blocks—the 350—was also introduced in 1967. On a more plebian level, the 307 was introduced in 1968 to replace the 283. Despite the appearance of the big-block 409 V-8 in 1962, and the other big-block engines that would follow, the small-block held its own surprisingly well. The small-block's output from mild to wild served a greater number of Chevrolet drivers.

The new generation of Corvette Sting Rays that made a debut in 1963 featured a new generation of small-blocks under the hood. This 1963 Corvette Z06 was the top of the line with the RPO Z06 special performance equipment option and the L84 327 ci V-8 small-block that pumped out 360 hp in fuel injected form. It was the dawn of a golden age. Jerry Heasley

The 327-ci V-8

The 283 V-8 had been released only a short time before the possibility of enlarging the small-block again was considered. Maurice Rosenberger remembered when the topic first arose.

"About that time, 1957, I knew a Cadillac-Olds-Chevy dealer in west Chicago that did a lot of roadraces running Chevy stuff," he said. "Of course, the Corvette had the V-8 by then and this man started working on them. He invited me to some of these races and we saw Lance Reventlow and Chuck Daigh racing oversized Chevy engines at 342 cubic inches when we had a 283. I think they bored them the limit and stroked them. I went over to see one of the races and Chuck Daigh was there, and they had several of those engines there. I became kind of impressed with the fact they were able to do that and make them run as well as they seemed to.

"I went back and told Cole about it and he said, 'Why don't you look at what manufacturing could get in this thing in the way of an enlarged displacement?' So they went to work and studied the thing with manufacturing and they came up with the 327."

Manufacturing, of course, included the foundries that would cast the block and the engine plants that would machine the block. If a much larger displacement engine wasn't feasible from a manufacturing standpoint within the block's current dimensions, there was no point in pursuing the project. The original block, remember, was designed for only 265 ci.

Cole was a firm believer in the short-stroke V-8 for a whole host of very good engineering reasons, so the increase would have to come from the bore as well as the stroke. The question was, could the 283 V-8's bore of 3.875 in. be increased without too many headaches?

"Cole came along and said he wanted a 4.00 in. bore in that engine," McPherson remembered. "As I recall, when I limit-stacked that engine, we had some walls .018 in. thick. There was a possibility of getting them that thin. That was a real challenge to the foundry, to improve their core-making capability and core-setting capability. We really never had trouble with the 4.00 in. bore because the foundry did a pretty good job in their limit-stack and control."

The 327 V-8 was the first small-block designed at the new Chevrolet Engineering Center. With all the facilities essentially under one roof, this new small-block could proceed from design to production with more efficiency, but the engine was not rushed into manufacture.

"What prompted the move to a larger displacement was an increase in the number of accessories and options that were power-driven," said Fred Sherman. "Power steering became much more popular. Air conditioning also became popular. You had to have more output to handle these things. The 348 cubic inch engine that came out in 1958 we had problems with. That was not a small-block. It was a completely different engine. You could get a small-block set up right that would just run all over that 348. Testing on the 327 began about a year and a half before its introduction in the 1962 model year."

Testing of the first batch of 327 blocks did reveal problems in controlling the placement of the cores during casting. Slight shifting of these cores subsequently resulted in increased oil consumption as a result of the thin cylinder wall deflection.

"The 327 finally reached a point where there was core shift with the cylinder bores," Sherman said. "There had been a problem with the 327 with oil consumption. Finally, they did come up with a fix and it was done by the Tonawanda engine plant. They increased the thickness from the top and bottom of the cylinder barrel of the block, and that solved the problem."

The 327 V-8 had a bore of 4.00 in. and a stroke of 3.25 in. It retained the main journal diameter of 2.30 in. and the rod journal diameter of 2.00 in. from the 283 V-8. Despite the bore and stroke differential, the 327 could share many of the components of the 283, and thus the cost of the engine could be kept down, costing only slightly more than the 283 V-8, with significantly more torque and horsepower.

There was a downside to using many of the components from the 283 V-8 in the 327, however. Dick Keinath recalled the development problems that arose in the pursuit of enlarging the small-block even further.

"We could install an experimental engine in a test car, give it to my boss, Mr. Duntov, he'd take it out to the Proving Grounds, take one lap around the track at full-throttle, then—boom!—there'd be a cloud of dust and pool of oil," Keinath recalled grimly. "You just don't do that to an engine you had put $100,000 into. As soon as you install a high-output camshaft, two four-barrels and high-output, large, ported, high-compression heads, the bottom would fall out.

"We worked very hard back then on crankshaft and connecting rod bearings because we were getting very high loads. You've got to remember that engine had been designed for 265 cubic inches with

The 1963 Corvette L84 engine with RPO Z06 provided a potent package. The standard carbureted small-block produced 300 or 340 hp depending on the cam, while the fuelie's output was a tire-melting 360 hp. Only 199 Corvettes were built in 1963 with RPO Z06. Jerry Heasley

a 2.00 in. diameter crankpin [rod journal] and a 2.30 in. diameter crankshaft main bearing. At that time we had to work very hard to get bearing materials to live on that size bearing. We finally increased the connecting rod journals to 2.10 in. and the main journals to 2.45 in. [in 1968] because the crankshafts were breaking and the bearings were failing. The crankshaft was just too flimsy, especially when we started to put in more horsepower. There was intensive development to make the engine live. That's why it took quite a while to go from 283 to 327."

Further Small-block Development

While the engine that would eventually become the 327 V-8 was being evaluated, further development was progressing on the small-block, primarily in the area of high performance. Dick Keinath was instrumental in these efforts during the late fifties and early sixties.

"In 1958 I was assigned to work as an engineer for Mr. Duntov," Keinath recalled. "At that time, Duntov had two engineers working for him—a chassis engineer and an engine engineer. I was the engine engineer and Harold Kreager was the chassis engineer. One of the first things I did for him was a hydraulic racing camshaft. I designed one, we built it, tested it—ran great. It never went into production because the racing boys preferred to adjust the valves. They didn't trust hydraulic lifters.

"While in Duntov's group, I bored out the 283 to 4.00 in. That was a 302. That one did not get into production as such because we used it as a tool. I loved it, Duntov loved it and we tried every which way to get it into production but it never made it. When we designed the 302 in 1958, the foundry couldn't make it. The foundry couldn't hold the cores to permit a 4-in. bore in 1958, but by 1961, they could.

"We did a lot of work on it strictly for Corvettes," Keinath continued. "In the laboratory we made camshafts for it, special carburetion, special manifolds, both inlet and exhaust, but what happened was that about a year later, we started working on the 327. So, the 327 came out after the 283 and before the 302, which eventually was offered in a special package—the Z-28.

"The other thing I worked on heavily with Duntov was an aluminum engine. We did aluminum blocks, heads, manifold, water pump and clutch housing. We were given the assignment to make aluminum work. At the time, we were working with high silicon aluminum for the cylinder heads. We tried to make it run without inserted valve seats and without inserted valve guides. We succeeded in making the cylinder head live but the valves wore out on the high silicon aluminum material. All this work was performed on 283s. The aluminum intake manifolds, aluminum clutch housing, and aluminum water outlet all entered production."

In 1960, Keinath moved to the production V-8 engine group, now under Don McPherson, and there were staff changes in Duntov's group. Although the aluminum small-block work in Duntov's group took place in the late fifties, this research and development had a dramatic impact on future small-block development in the sixties. In addition, racers and performance enthusiasts desired the parts they knew Chevrolet was developing. A system had to be established to get these parts out. Once again, Cole was instrumental in this all-important phase of the small-block's rising popularity.

Interior of the 1963 Corvette was still a blend of stylish curves and gleaming chrome, highly developed from the 1958 version but still showing its roots. Jerry Heasley

Performance Parts Development

Bill Howell began work in Chevrolet's engine test laboratory in 1961, and got to work closely with both the production engine group and Duntov's performance engine group.

"Basically, they had two groups that worked on the small-block at the time," he said. The basic production engine group developed the hardware—cylinder blocks and so forth—and Zora Duntov's group was involved in high-performance hardware, basically for the Corvette. The majority of the high-performance work on the small-block up through 1965 was done by the Corvette group. Zora's philosophy was that everything that he did in the way of high performance had to be streetable. He would not let you develop a camshaft that could not be driven on the street."

Nevertheless, there were high-performance racing parts for the small-block disbursed through SEDCO, the Southern Engineering Development Co., established by Vince Piggins under the direction of Piggins' boss, Walt MacKenzie, who was a Chevrolet staff engineer.

The Camaro was the first and only Chevrolet to receive the 350 V-8 introduced in 1967. The RPO number was L48 as offered in the SS 350 Camaro that year. It was rated at 295 hp. The 350 V-8 was introduced first as a high performance engine, then later offered in detuned versions for other Chevrolet models. Chevrolet

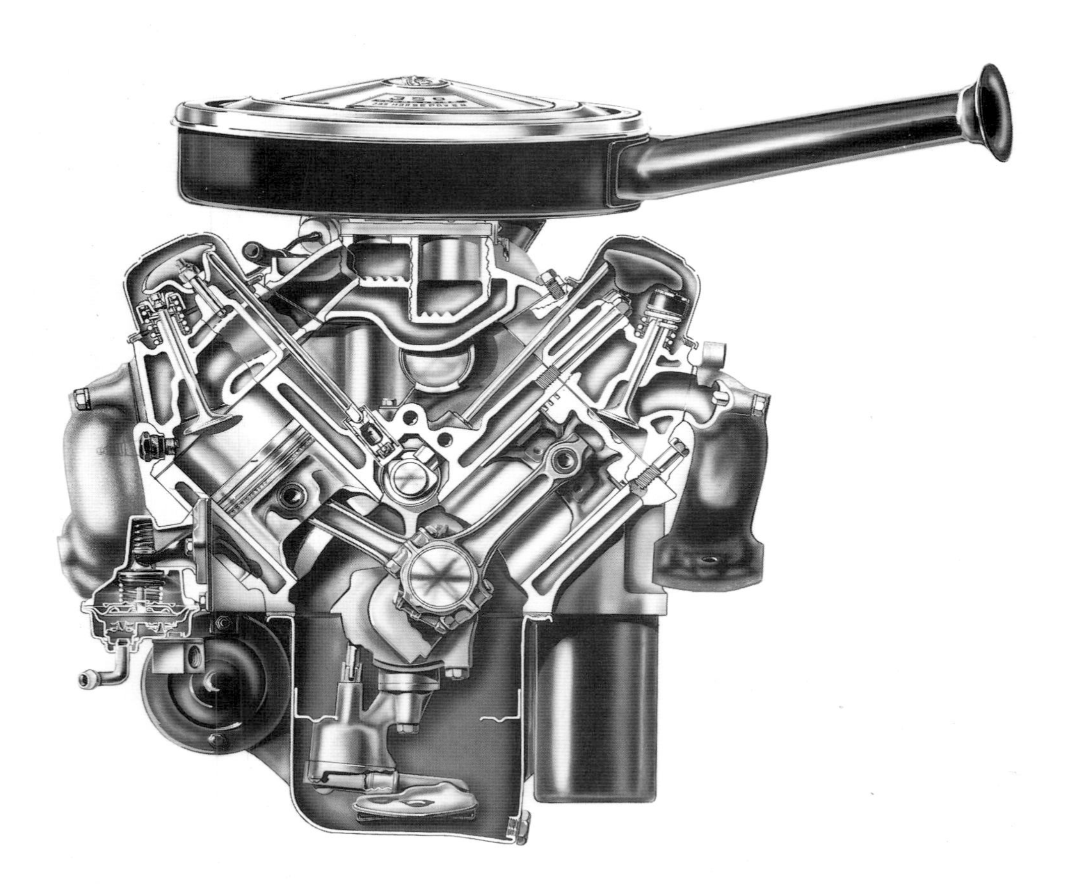

The 350 V-8 was introduced in 1967. It featured a 4.00 in. bore and a 3.48 in. stroke. Production of this engine now numbers in the millions. It has adapted beautifully to all horsepower, emissions and economy requirements placed on it. Chevrolet

SEDCO was a wonderfully low-profile means of meeting racers' needs without too much fanfare.

Paul Prior became involved with this activity, and for him and others it was an off-again, on-again endeavor, rising and falling with the whims of Chevrolet upper management.

"My brother was an engineer at the GM Proving Grounds and he told me of an opening, so I applied for it and got it. Less that a year later, in 1951, Walt MacKenzie needed a couple of guys. He came out and interviewed myself and another fellow and we both went to work for him. He needed technical writers, so I was a technical writer for a few years. Starting in 1955, when Chevrolet first had to pay attention to performance, the performance activity was instituted under MacKenzie. Technically, I was not in that activity then, but MacKenzie knew I had a great interest in it, so I did some peripheral things with them then, and that's when I first got to know Vince Piggins.

"The AMA (Automobile Manufacturers Association) ban of 1957 put the lid on racing and promotion of Chevrolet's success, and the activities of the small performance group came to a near standstill. Vince became a service engineer for trucks and I kept plodding along with tech writing.

"It doesn't matter whether you have an annointed group or not to handle performance," Prior said of the nearcessation of racing promotion and parts supply. "People on the outside are going to do it anyway and they are going to contact whoever they can at the company. When it's somewhat disorganized like that, then some stuff starts slipping out the back door that probably shouldn't, and it becomes a poorly administered effort. This, no doubt, was going on.

"In the spring of 1960, Cole decided that there should be some central activity to clear this type of thing. Vince was pulled out of truck service and I became his assistant. Early in 1961, Doug Roe came into the group. He had been a development engineer at the Proving Grounds. For years, it was then Vince, me and Doug."

That small group was called "Product Performance." It has gone by various names over the years since, but the basic principle of developing performance parts and getting them to racers and enthusiasts hasn't changed. With Cole's decision to promote Chevrolet's performance, high-performance engine and parts development took on a renewed priority.

"We spent an awful lot of our time on performance development," McPherson concurred. "That was a large part of the sales pitch that Cole wanted when he was general manager. He wanted to win the races. He wanted to be in all the available races for that class of engine. We spent a great deal of time, effort and money making sure that engine was well ahead of the competition—which it always was."

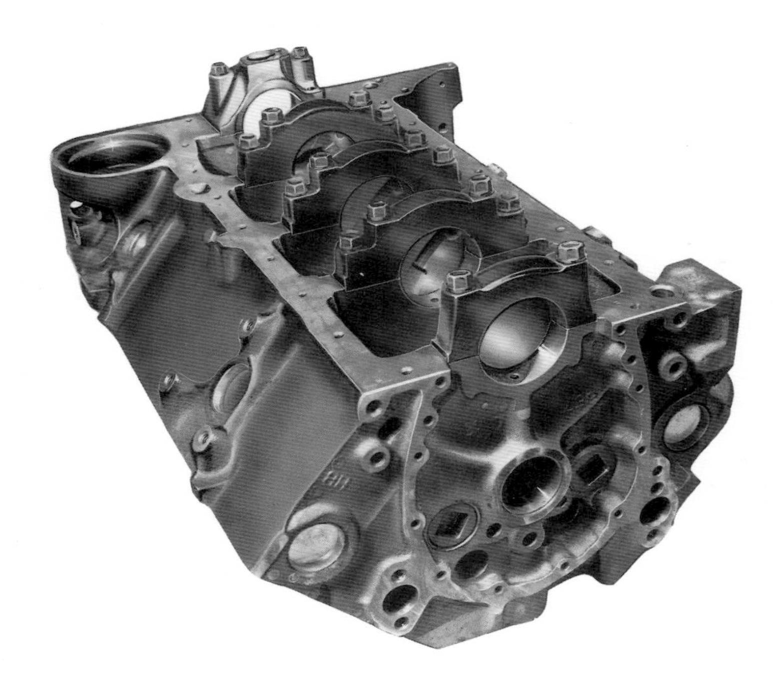

The 4.00 in. bore small-block was the first to receive four-bolt main bearing caps for high-performance applications and use with nodular iron crankshafts. These included certain versions of the 302 and 350, but the 327 was only offered with a two-bolt block. Chevrolet

Cowl Air Induction

In the summer of 1962, Vince Piggins began a series of tests to determine why racing stock cars in general, and Chevrolet in particular, couldn't maintain consistent top speed, and why their performance decreased slightly as the race wore on during a typical NASCAR event. The outcome of these tests would not only have a dramatic impact on stock car racing, but street performance cars as well. In fact, the results would, in time, affect the entire automobile manufacturing industry. The small-block, as well as the big-block, would directly be affected in Chevrolet's future product offerings.

In July 1962, Piggins sent driver Rex White and mechanic Louie Clemens to Daytona Speedway to conduct these tests. Doug Roe was also assigned to the test program. Specifically, Piggins wanted to find out why a production Chevrolet Biscayne 409 was nearly 2 mph slower than a Pontiac 380 having twenty-five less horsepower.

"In conducting these tests," Piggins wrote in a paper to this author in 1977, titled, "Carburetor Cold Air Induction", he stated "complete underhood environmental conditions were monitored in numerous locations, including the cowl plenum area that provides fresh air to the passenger compartment. Digesting and comparing the Chevrolet/Pontiac data, it was immediately evident that conditions within the Pontiac engine compartment were both lower in temperature and slightly high pressure-wise in the immediate air cleaner area.

"To simulate this condition at the carburetor, an air scoop was fashioned from an extra flywheel housing cover, and attached to the Chevy hood over a hole connected to the carburetor intake. This

The high performance 302 V-8 was first offered in the 1967 Z/28 Camaro, which was the engine's RPO number. It was rated at 290 hp but this was a conservative rating. Displacement was achieved by putting a 283 crankshaft in the 327 engine block. The high-revving 302 was happier on the track than the street. Chevrolet

While RPO Z06 provided a standard option race package for the Corvette, the base L84-engined Corvette was no slouch. This white split-window Sting Ray coupe was available with either a four-speed manual or Powerglide automatic transmission coupled to the 327 ci small-block. Musclecar Review

High-performance small-block development in the sixties was truly exotic. This partially assembled 327/377 engine shows the gear-driven single overhead camshaft with roller rocker arms. Denny Davis

modification immediately increased the Chevy's top speed by 3½ to 4 mph per lap. Air pressure at the carburetor was raised to a level comparable to that of the Pontiac. The big change, however, was the carburetor air temperature being lowered from a previous 124 degrees to 89 degrees. It was immediately evident that the complaint by many stock car drivers of being unable to maintain a lap speed within one or two miles per hour of their first qualifying lap [sic]. Obviously with underhood air intake, as the engine compartment temperature rose, the speed and power decreased."

This was a dramatic finding. Piggins suggested the immediate design, release and production of a special edition fresh air hood for the 1963 Chevrolet Biscayne, but major sheetmetal changes like this were prohibitive and required long lead times to produce. Fresh air hood induction on street Chevys would have to wait several years, but the results of the findings immediately found their way into Chevrolet stock cars that used a special air cleaner that drew cool outside air from the cowl plenum. This set a precedent copied by every other NASCAR competitor.

"In June of 1965," Piggins wrote, "the first hood with an integral cold air system was designed for the Corvette. This design modified the 1966 Corvette hood, using a "do it yourself" instruction sheet for Corvette owners. A few cuts with a sabre saw, and fabrication in fiberglass of an air box plenum surrounding the carburetor air cleaner and you had your fresh air hood. To eliminate water entry, bugs, etc., the intake was directed forward from a high pressure area at the windshield base.

"In 1967, the Corvette offered an optional fresh air hood of similar design for use with the L-88 [small-block] engine option. This was probably the first production available use of performance hoods in the industry."

Fresh air hoods became optional on the Camaro Z-28 as well as the Chevelle. It soon became mandatory that any performance car out of Detroit had to have some form of fresh air induction. Later still, this concept would help car manufacturers not only meet emissions requirements, but boost performance as well.

The Rise of the 327

The 327 V-8 featured greatly in Chevrolet's performance plans in the early to mid-sixties, while the 283 V-8 was now looked upon as essentially a medium-duty passenger car engine. Consequently, the emphasis on small-block performance development shifted to the 327, and horsepower levels of this engine reached breath-taking heights during the sixties.

In its first year of production, 1962, the 327 was offered in four different levels of power. The 250-hp Turbo-Fire 327 came with a four-barrel carburetor, a 10.5:1 compression ratio and dual exhaust. This was the standard V-8 in the Corvette.

There were three optional 327 V-8s. The 300-hp Turbo-Fire 327 used larger, 1.94 in.-diameter intake valves, as opposed to the 1.75 in.-diameter intake valves in the 250-hp 327 V-8; a larger carburetor, having the same compression ratio, cost only $53.80 more.

The L84 Corvette engine was avant garde for its time with the beautifully finished fuel-injection block and valve covers. Musclecar Review

The 302 as installed in the Z/28. This engine is fitted with the belt-driven air pump (mounted between the valve cover and air cleaner) as part of the Air Injection Reactor emissions control system necessary to meet California's stringent emissions standards in the late sixties. The date on the fan shroud reads 12-9-67. Chevrolet

Zora Arkus-Duntov was at work again in 1962-1963 creating a full-race lightweight Corvette to beat the Ferraris and Jaguars on the track. He had plans to build 125 of his Grand Sport Corvettes, but when Chevrolet brass found out that he was working against the 1957 AMA ban on racing that was still in effect, the Grand Sport program was cancelled and only five cars were finished. While the Grand Sports used several engines over the years, the most exciting was a modified small-block with lightweight aluminum cylinder heads and cross-ram intake manifold that displaced 377 ci. This special engine was reported to make 435 lb-ft of torque at 4000 rpm and 485 hp at 6000 rpm. Chevrolet

The 307 ci V-8 was first offered in 1968 to replace the 283 V-8, which was discontinued with the 1967 model year. The 307 had the same 3.87 in. bore as the 283 but a longer 3.25 in. stroke, for an actual displacement of 306.6 ci. The 307 was offered through the 1973 model year. It was only offered with a two-barrel carburetor. Note the exhaust manifold Air Injection Reactor system to improve exhaust emissions. Chevrolet

Next came the 340-hp version with dual four-barrel carburetors and a more radical camshaft, costing $107.60 over the base V-8. Finally, there was the 360-hp fuel-injected 327 with an 11.25:1 compression ratio, costing $484.00. These last two engines were reserved only for the Corvette.

The 300-hp 327 V-8 was the highest-output small-block available in the full-size Chevrolets; if you wanted more power, the big-block 409 V-8 took over. Chevrolet's new Chevy II did not have factory-installed optional V-8s, but did have a factory-offered kit permitting the dealer to install either a 283 or 327 small-block V-8.

Small-block engine specifications remained virtually unchanged for 1963. *Road & Track* finally had an opportunity to road test a new, rebodied '63 Corvette. The car had the optional L84 360-hp fuel-injected 327 with four-speed manual transmission. This Corvette reached 60 mph in 5.9 seconds, covered the quarter-mile in 14.5 seconds at 95 mph, and had a top speed of 142 mph.

In 1964, the magazine tested a Corvette with the 300-hp 327 and 2-speed Powerglide automatic transmission. The car reached 60 mph in a more leisurely 8.0 seconds, covered the quarter-mile in 15.2 seconds at 85 mph, and had a top speed of 130 mph.

There was a slight boost in the optional 327 V-8's performance for 1964. The 300-hp L75 V-8 with a single, four-barrel carburetor remained in the lineup. Output of the L76 was raised from 340 hp to 365 hp, achieved with a single, four-barrel carburetor, and still costing only $107.60. The fuel-injected L84 327 V-8 developed 375 hp; you could have it for $538.00

There were no specification changes in the 327's standard and optional engines for 1965, but there was the availability of big-block power in the Corvette—the 396 V-8. Still, the level of power could be dialed in to the small-block that was more than adequate in keeping pace with the bigger and heavier 396 V-8 and later the 427 V-8. However, the arrival of the new big-blocks would cause Chevrolet to limit the number of optional 327s in 1966. In 1965, there were four optional 327 V-8s in the Corvette: the 300-hp L75, the 350-hp L79, the 365-hp L76 and the 375-hp L84. In 1966, there was only one optional 327 V-8 in the Corvette—the L79.

The free-breathing cylinder heads on the high-performance 302 were a key to the engine's high output. The Z/28 302 was offered in 1967, 1968 and 1969 and was rated at 290 hp all three years. Chevrolet

For 1966, the output of the L30 327 V-8 offered in the Chevy II, Chevelle and full-size Chevrolet was increased from 250 hp to 275 hp. This was the only optional 327 V-8 offered in the full-size Chevrolet. In the Chevy II or Chevelle that year, you could get the L30 or L79 small-block 327. Availability of the small-block as a factory-installed option in the Chevy II had been a reality for several years, and the L79 turned the 1966 Chevy II into a screamer on the street—or strip, for that matter. Of course, if the prospective buyers of these cars didn't want this level of power, the trusty 283 V-8 with 220 hp could be ordered by just checking off RPO L77.

Chevrolet had not been idly looking for other means by which to expand the small-block's abilities. The division had been hard at work looking at displacements both smaller and greater than the venerable 327 V-8. Two new small-block V-8s were offered for 1967: the 302 as installed in the new Camaro Z-28, and the 350 V-8 available only in the Camaro SS350.

The Z-28 302-ci V-8

As every Chevrolet enthusiast knows, the Camaro Z-28 was conceived by Vince Piggins to compete in the SCCA Trans-Am series. Both the car and the engine were designed by a very capable

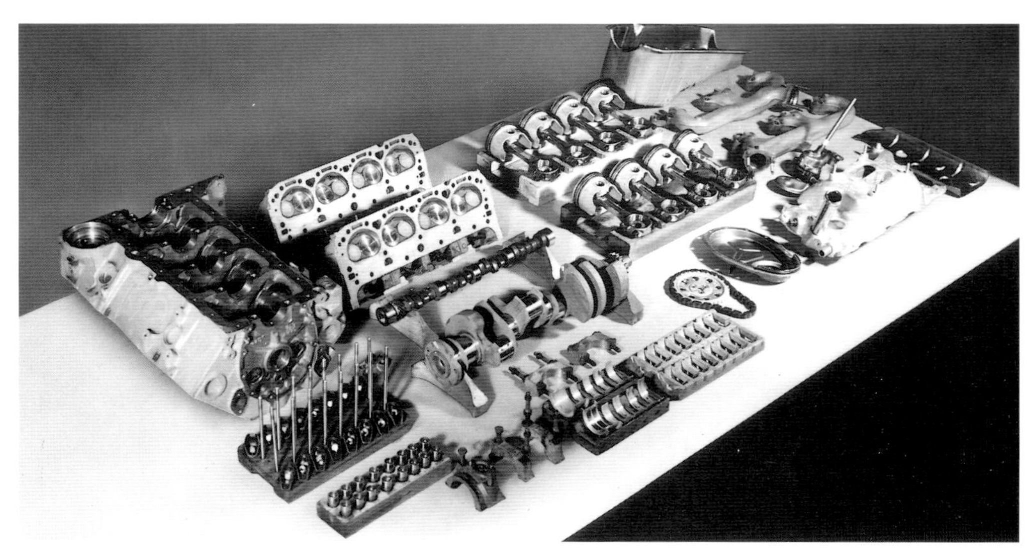

All the components in the 1967 Z/28 were strictly high performance. The crankshaft, pistons and connecting rods were forged. Intake valves measured 2.02 in., exhaust valves were 1.60 in. The camshaft was mechanical. The 1967 engine block, as shown in this photo, featured two-bolt main bearings. Four-bolt mains were used in 1968 and 1969. Chevrolet

sweepstakes hands-down, even before the light turned green.

Car and Driver tested a 1967 Z-28 and achieved a 0-to-60 mph time of 6.7 seconds, covering the quarter-mile in 14.9 seconds at 97 mph. The editors had this to say about the car: "The engine is obviously the Z-28's strongest point . . . The 290-hp figure quoted for the Z-28 engine seems ridiculously conservative; it feels at least as strong as the 327 ci, 350-hp hydraulic-lifter engine offered in the Corvette.

"The 302 engine is without a doubt the most responsive American V-8 we've ever tested, although there is a trace of unevenness at low speeds because of the carburetor's unusually large venturi area. Once it begins to pull, however, it smooths out and lunges forward like a 426 Hemi. The red-line on the tach was at 5500 rpm, which we and the engine cheerfully ignored. It revs quickly to 6000 rpm, with no sign of getting tight, and we reluctantly shifted—in the interests of prudence."

There was another new Camaro model for 1967, and it too was based on its new engine: the Camaro SS350. This was a new small-block V-8, and it, too, went through its share of development problems before seeing the production light of day.

The L48 350 ci Turbo-Fire small-block of the 1967 Camaro SS. The Camaro SS was also available with the new Chevrolet big-block in either 325 or 375 hp form—the latter at almost double the price of the small-block. Musclecar Review

The 350-ci V-8

Although Ed Cole had not been general manager of Chevrolet since 1961, having moved up the GM corporate ladder, he still had strong ties to the division and was very much interested in the small-block's state of health and future. In fact, he was involved in the next step in the small-block's evolution.

In 1965, when the possibility of enlarging the small-block was considered, Don McPherson was assistant chief engineer of passenger cars. It was a time of tremendous growth and activity at Chevrolet, with two new models added to the Chevrolet lineup, the Chevy II and the Chevelle, and another new one, the Camaro, in the works. Engine development work was also accelerating, and the future 350-ci V-8 would be part of that hectic activity.

"Cole came along one day," McPherson remembered, "and got ahold of me and said, 'I want to go to 350 cubic inches and I want it all in bore.' It took me about a month and a half to collar him and show

Interior of the 1967 Camaro SS 350 with the tachometer and speedometer well-placed for performance driving. This car has the optional Powerglide automatic transmission installed. Musclecar Review

The car that brought fame to the Camaro Z/28, the Mark Donohue-Roger Penske Trans-Am Sunoco Camaro. The team swept the series in 1968 and again in 1969. The car has been painstakingly restored and still competes today in vintage racing and Trans-Am reunions.

him a layout proving it was pretty tough to have the pistons overlap one another. I said, 'Where do you want the flat spots on the rings?' He didn't like the sarcasm, but I said, 'we're just going to have to leave the 4.00 inch bore and stroke it,' and that's what we did."

The task of designing the 350 V-8 fell to Dick Keinath and his V-8 engine group. It involved much more work than either the 283 or the 327 had to undergo. It was no simple matter of increasing the stroke from 3.25 in. to 3.48 in.

"That was one engine where we had quite an argument going on whether we would be successful in getting that much displacement out of a small-block casting," Keinath recalled vividly. "We agreed at the time that we were going to do it, but we were going to keep it as a passenger car version and try not to hot-rod it, because we didn't think it would live. And, of course, the argument always was, 'Once you get it out there, we're going to end up hot-rodding it because we always do.' No matter what management assured me that they would avoid giving me a lot of problems, performance and durability-wise, we engineers down on the firing line felt that we were going to have to make it live regardless, so we just kept working hard on it.

"We raised the lower portion of the bore and made sure that there was enough room to swing the crankshaft in the panrail area because we needed to get a better connecting rod in there. With a high stroke, we were throwing the piston off pretty fast and we needed to get a little more material into the connecting rod, which increased rotating and reciprocating weight. That meant we had to put bigger counterweights on the crankshaft, which meant we had to make sure there was room to swing the bigger counterweights, which in essence reduced the frequency of the crankshaft and made it more vulnerable to torsional breakage."

In an effort to alleviate these anticipated problems, the crankshaft journal diameters were increased for the first time since the small-block was introduced. Main journal diameter was increased to 2.45 in. and rod journal diameter was increased to 2.10 in. Unlike the 302 crankshaft, the 350 V-8 used a cast nodular iron crankshaft, and thus didn't receive the Tufftriding process. It was considered perfectly adequate for use in anticipated passenger cars, but Keinath's worst fears were realized when he learned the 350 V-8 would make its debut in none other than a high-performace Camaro model, the SS350.

Interestingly, output of the 350 V-8 in the Camaro SS350 would not approach the levels of the optional, smaller-displacement 327 V-8 used in the Corvette. It was rated at 295 hp at 4800 rpm with 380 pounds-feet of torque at 3200 rpm. Compression ratio was 10.25:1, the camshaft was hydraulic and the engine was fed by a single four-barrel Rochester carburetor. In this state of tune, there should not have been problems, but there were, almost from the time the Camaro SS350 was put into the hands of eager buyers.

Joe Bertsch joined Chevrolet in 1955. He was involved in projects ranging from the Level-Air suspension and Corvair engine cooling to work on the straight-six engine. He became first-line supervisor of the V-8 engine group in 1968. When the problems with the 350 V-8 first arose, it was Bertsch's job to find a satisfactory and quick solution.

"We had problems on the 350 V-8 after the engine went into production," Bertsch said, "where the crankshaft nose would break off, the torsional damper would fall off and the number one arm would break. There was a lot of hollering about that, believe me! We fixed the problem in production within a month. We solved the crankshaft problem by press-fitting on the torsional damper and putting a drawbolt in the nose of the crank. That preloaded the fillet where the nose turned down to the number one main journal, and reduced cyclic stress. In addition to that, we had to revise the arm section of the number one arm and beef it up by adding arm width and material."

Working out early production problems of the 350 V-8 was not out of the ordinary, because all new and existing engines were under constant development or improvement.

"Typically, new passenger car engine development is four or five years ahead of production," Howell said. "The other

In 1967, labels appeared underhood to help mechanics maintain proper engine tune to reduce emissions. Instructions listed proper settings for carburetor mixture, ignition timing and idle setting. The engine in the photo is a 275 hp Turbo-Fire 327 V-8. Chevrolet

Next page
For 1969, the Camaro was subtly redesigned and became the highest-selling first-generation Camaro. The Z/28 option was basically a homologation special to allow the Camaro to be eligible for Trans-Am racing. Musclear Review

GOODYEAR
GT RADIAL
GOODYEAR
RADIAL

Z/28

The RPO Z/28 package for 1969 included the 302 ci small-block with bright accents and dual exhausts. Inside the engine, the 302 received four-bolt main bearings, which help produce 290 hp from the small engine. Musclecar Review

The subtle restyling to the Camaro body in 1969 continued in the interior and dashboard arrangement. This is the controls of the Z/28. Musclecar Review

interest in passenger car engine development is, after you develop a package that does so much and costs so much, you ask, 'Well, how can I do the same less expensively?' So you have a great deal of passenger car engine development in the form of durability testing, where you're testing new components that cost less money.

"The laboratory at Chevrolet was divided up into six or eight development dyno cells and six or eight durability cells. It was not unusual for the durability stuff to run six days a week, twenty-four hours a day. Each cell had a soundproof operating room, a six-by-twelve-foot bedplate with the dynamometer mounted in the middle of it. Typically, you could run two engines on it but you could only run them one at a time.

"One whole side of the lab building was machine shop. On the other side were the test facilities. In between the two was the motor room. Typically, everything that was run in the lab was built and qualified in the motor room and after the engine was tested it was torn down in the motor room for inspection. They had their own assemblers, disassemblers and inspectors."

Car & Driver managed to get an early production 1967 Camaro SS350 to test. Straight-line performance was not up to par with other performance Chevys. With a four-speed manual transmission and 3.31:1 rear end ratio, the car reached 60 mph in 7.8 seconds and covered the quarter-mile in 16.1 seconds at a leisurely 86.5 mph. This was partially due to severe wheel hop, a problem that was resolved in later production cars with the addition of a traction bar.

Hot Rod tested the Camaro SS350 and got significantly better results. The difference between the two cars was a 3.55:1 rear end ratio, the addition of the traction bar, and a Bill Thomas dyno-tune. Best quarter-mile time was 14.85 seconds at 95 mph—much more in keeping with the car's image.

The Camaro, then, had an embarrassment of riches in 1967 when it came to small-block power. The standard base (no extra cost) V-8 was the 210-hp 327 V-8. Optional small-blocks included the Z-28 302 V-8 or the SS350 V-8—essentially vehicle/engine packages. If you wanted more, there was the big-block 325-hp or 375-hp 396 V-8.

In the Chevy II, the base engines were the in-line four- and six-cylinder

The Chevrolet small-block was the engine of choice for 1960s American racers, whether it was stuffing a homegrown V-8 into a Ferrari or Maserati, or using it to power a homebuilt sports racer such as the fiberglass body kit Devin. In 1962, race-car builder Bill Thomas developed the Cheetah around the small-block. The Cheetah was based on a sprint-car-type tube-frame chassis with lightweight aluminum sports-car bodywork. The 327 ci engine was placed in front but mounted behind the front axle to balance weight. While Thomas had plans for full street and race-car production, GM corporate politics and race organization homologation rulers blocked his progress. David Gooley

The Chevrolet small-block V-8 was the foundation of the Chaparral, America's greatest race car bar none. Texas oilman Jim Hall built his first, front-engined Chaparrals based on the old Scarab. By the early 1960s, Hall developed the second generation of Chaparrals as mid-engined, fiberglass bodied racers that would eventually clean up in racing from sports cars to sports prototypes to Can Am. The Chaparrals were continuously updated and rebuilt, often using the same chassis. This is an early Chaparral 2 in 1990s vintage race form. Chevrolet

By 1965, the Chaparral 2 had gone several stages further in development. The suspension and wheels were all Chaparral team work and miles ahead of the competition. The early front air dam and rear spoilers were also Chaparral ideas that would forever change the way the rest of the world looked at aerodynamics. The early Chaparrals were all built around special 327 ci aluminum small-blocks while the later cars were powered by 427 ci big-blocks. Chevrolet

The Chaparral 2D was updated for endurance racing with a fully enclosed cockpit, overhead air intake scoop to feed the mid-mounted engine and larger rear spoilers. With the aluminum 327 ci small-block, the 2D won the 1966 Nurburgring long-distance race at the hands of drivers Jo Bonnier and Phil Hill. Chevrolet

engines and the optional V-8 was the L30 275-hp 327.

The full-size Chevrolet for 1967 had the 195-hp 283 V-8 as the standard V-8, but this was to be the last year for this engine in the Chevrolet lineup. The only optional small-block was the 275-hp 327 V-8. Big-block fans could order the 396 or the 427 V-8.

The Corvette for 1967 again came standard with the 300-hp 327 V-8. Because of the plethora of optional 396 and 427 V-8s, the only optional small-block was the L-97 350-hp 327.

The 283 V-8 had had a long life for a small-block—1957 through 1967. Chevrolet introduced a new displacement engine to replace it for 1968.

The 307

With all the demands being placed on it in the later sixties, the 283 V-8 was in need of revitalization. In the minds of many car buyers at the time, a V-8 engine under 300 ci was perceived as too small. At the same time, these buyers viewed the 327 as a performance V-8, which it was, and it was more powerful than these buyers needed.

To fill this perceived need, Chevrolet chose to install a 327 V-8 crankshaft in

The CERV I and II were two further experiments by Zora Arkus-Duntov to stretch the envelope of Chevrolet performance based on the small-block. The CERV I began life in 1959 as a 283 ci, mid-engined single-seater. The CERV II shown here was created in 1963 as a mid-engined prototype intended for sports prototype racing at Le Mans and Daytona. Power came from an aluminum-head 377 ci engine, as used in the Grand Sport. Both cars remained prototypes. Chevrolet

the 283 block. Bore and stroke was thus 3.875 x 3.25 in. to achieve a displacement of 307 ci. This simple crankshaft swap cost little, and solved Chevrolet's standard V-8 image dilemma. In addition, this was the large-journal crankshaft with 2.45 in. main journals and 2.10 in. rod journals, so it was sturdier than the 283.

It was decided this new V-8 would remain a two-barrel carburetor engine. Compression ratio was 9.0:1. The engine was rated at 200 hp at 4600 rpm.

Unlike the 283, 327 and 350 that came before the 307, Chevrolet did no performance development on the 307, so there were no performance versions of this engine. It wasn't even available with a four-barrel carburetor. The beauty of the small-block's design, however, was that performance could easily be increased with a simple intake manifold and carburetor swap.

The 307 V-8 served base V-8 duty in the full-size Chevrolets, Chevelles and Chevy IIs.

Lola Cars of England built special formula cars, sports racing prototypes and Can Am cars beginning in the late 1950s. The great Lola T-70 was first constructed in 1965 and originally built around the Aston Martin V-8 or the Ford small-block V-8. But as the Chevrolet small-block provided more power with less weight, Lola soon switched over. This T-70 is being prepped to hit the grid for a vintage race. David Gooley

The 1968 Lineup

The biggest change in small-block specifications for 1968 was the switch to larger 2.45 in. main journals and 2.10 in. rod journals. All small-blocks benefitted, including the 302, 307, 327 and 350 V-8s.

For 1968, Chevrolet expanded availability of the 350 V-8 to the Chevy II. A Nova SS option, L48, put the 295-hp 350 V-8 into the two-door V-8 series Chevy II for $210.65. (The RPO L30 250-hp 327 V-8 was dropped.) Chevrolet advertised the availability of the 350 V-8 in its stylish compact with its "Chevy II much" ad that appeared in the enthusiast magazines that year. The ad read: "Topside, it's a neat little two-door. Underneath, it's all set to move. Beefed-up suspension, wide-oval red stripes and one of the greatest V-8s you've ever ordered into action. It's a 350-cu. in. 295-hp affair with 4-barrel carburetor and 2½" dual exhausts. Nova SS. We call it Chevy II much. You'll second the motion."

In the full-size Chevrolet that year, the standard 307 V-8 could be replaced by the optional 250-hp 327 with 8.75:1 cr or the 275-hp 327 with 10.0:1 cr. The 350 V-8 was still not available. One had to move up to big-block power if more horsepower was desired.

For the newly restyled Corvette, 1968 would be the last year for the 327. The 300-hp 327 was again standard. The only

The fuel-injection era that began in 1957 ended in 1965 with the 327 ci V-8. It was a refinement of earlier systems but was still an airflow-controlled, continuous-flow design. The most powerful version was rated at 375 hp at 6200 rpm and gave the Corvette awesome performance. Pictured here is the 360 hp version. Chevrolet

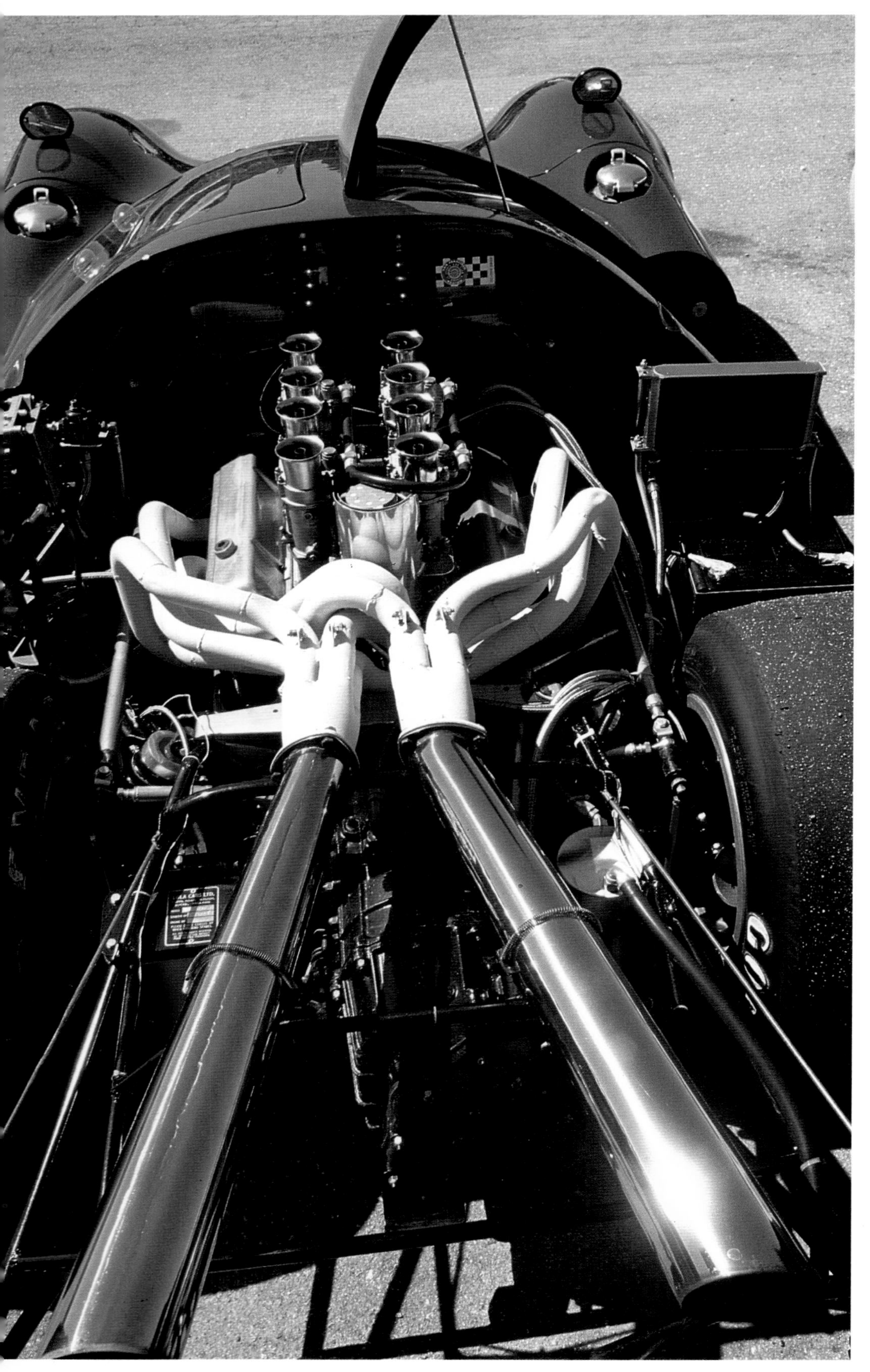

Iso Rivolta serial number 718, which raced at Le Mans in 1968 with a balanced and blue-printed 327 ci small-block producing 365 hp through a ZF five-speed. Special components included Iso connecting rods and oil pan. Winston Goodfellow

With the rear-end bodywork removed from the Lola T-70, all the glory of the special header and exhaust system is visible. Note the side-mounted radiators, which are fed air through vents above the doors. David Gooley

optional small-block was, as in 1967, RPO L79, the 350-hp 327 V-8.

Road & Track had never tested the 350-hp 327, but got a chance to in 1968 in a new Corvette. The car was equipped with a Muncie four-speed manual transmission and a 3.70:1 rear end ratio. The magazine had this to say about the most powerful 327 small-block available that year: "Though it isn't a new engine now, the 350-hp 327 is one that we've never road tested. Though it doesn't make such a production of idling as the hot 427, it isn't exactly smooth and quiet about it either. But it does run pretty quietly and tractably at anything above about 1200 rpm, and it has the distinct advantage of not adding 150 pounds to the Corvette's already gross avoirdupois. Fuel consumption is more reasonable too, at 13 mpg. But compared with the standard 300-bhp engine it is sluggish until it's over 3000 rpm. Reason: the 300 develops 360 lb-ft of torque at 3200 rpm, and the 350 develops the same maximum torque at a higher 3600 rpm. If it's instant response you want, get the 300; if it's shifting, get the 350."

The editors got the 350-hp Corvette to 60 mph in 7.7 seconds, and through the quarter-mile timing lights in 15.6 seconds at 92 mph.

In the Camaro camp for 1968, engine availability and specifications remained unchanged. The base V-8 was still the 210-hp 327. The Z-28 and SS350 options continued unchanged.

For the July 1968 issue of *Car & Driver*, the editors did a comparison test between a "tunnel-port" Mustang and a Z-28 with special, dealer-installed options. These options included: two 600-cfm Holley carburetors in a staggered configuration on top of a plenum manifold; special air cleaner for fresh air induction; rear axle assembly with disc brakes; special front disc brake assemblies; Koni shock absorbers; exhaust headers; heavy-duty valve springs; special distributor with transistorized ignition; and heavy-duty clutch and flywheel. The price of these dealer-installed options was $1731.80 over and above the Z-28 price of $3708.58. It was really a setup for road racing and less than practical on the street.

Next page
Italian industrialist Renzo Rivolta of Milan founded the Iso company in the late 1940s to produce motorscooters. By 1962, he had graduated to building exotic sports cars and sedans to compete with Ferrari, Maserati and Lamborghini. But instead of designing and building his own engine, Rivolta imported Chevrolet small-blocks for his cars, often tuning them for more power. The Iso Rivolta was Iso's first model, built 1962-1970, with some 800 made and many imported into the United States. Winston Goodfellow

With the Rivolta rolling off the production line, Iso turned to building a sports car, which it called the Iso Grifo A3. The Grifos were developed by Italian engineer Giotto Bizzarrini, who was famous for his work in creating the great Ferrari 250 GTO. The A3/C competition Grifos, such as this 1964 model, were raced from Le Mans to Daytona based on a front-mounted 327 ci small-block with a single four-barrel carburetor. With the single carburetor, the engine produced 365 hp, but mounted with Weber carburetors, it created 405-410 hp in race trim. Winston Goodfellow Collection

One of the secrets beneath the hood of the Iso Grifo A3 was the mounting of the 327 ci Corvette small-block engine. The engine was pushed way back from the front of the car to be mounted as close to the center as possible, resulting in what was essentially a mid-engined car with the engine in front of the driver versus behind. Inside the car, this also resulted in a large central tunnel for the transmission taking up a good portion of the interior room. This is a 1965 A3 Grifo street version, packing 365 hp. Winston Goodfellow Collection

After Sam Posey pushed both cars to their limits around the Lime Rock, Connecticut, race track, the editors took the cars to the drag strip. Both cars were very evenly matched. The Mustang reached 60 mph in 5.4 seconds, the Z-28 in 5.3 seconds. It took 12.5 seconds for the Mustang to reach 100 mph; the Z-28 did it in 12.3 seconds. Ford's ponycar covered the quarter-mile in 13.96 seconds at 106.13 mph and the Camaro did it in 13.77 seconds at 107.39 mph.

For all intents and purposes, these were race cars. No production street cars could match these times—except maybe Cobras. This was not the mainstream for the performance enthusiast, anyway. And for the Chevy enthusiast, there was much to choose from the last year of the decade.

The Small-block in 1969

This was the last year the 327 V-8 was available. The two-barrel version with 9.0:1 cr developing 235 hp was now the base V-8 engine in the full-size line of cars. The 307, with essentially the same specifications, was rated at 200 hp in the V-8 Chevelle series. The 200-hp 307 was also the base V-8 used in the Nova this year. In the Camaro, the base V-8 327 engine was rated at 210 hp.

In terms of optional small-blocks available in the full-size Chevrolet, there was the 255 hp (RPO LM1) or 300 hp (RPO L48) versions of the 350 V-8. These two optional engines were also available in the Chevelle and the Nova.

This was the third and last year for the 302-ci Z-28 V-8 option in the Camaro; a more potent 350 V-8 would replace it in 1970. The LM1 was available as an option or the 300-hp 350 V-8 could be acquired as part of the Z27 SS350 package.

In the Corvette for 1969, the standard engine was the 300-hp L48 350 V-8. The only small-block optional engine was the L46 350-hp 350 V-8.

This was a year of flux for the small-block Chevrolet V-8. The 302 and 327 were dropped at the end of the model year; new versions of the 350 V-8 were offered or were in the works; and there were rumors that a new, even *bigger* small-block was going to be announced for 1970. "How could the small-block go any further in displacement?" many asked. Still, the rumors were true.

As it would turn out, the small-block in the seventies would start with a bang and end with a whimper.

The Iso Grifo was redesigned in 1965 as more of a berlinetta. Meanwhile Giotto Bizzarrini set up his own car company in Livorno to build the old-style Grifos as Bizzarrini Grifos, which later became both the Strada and the GT America. This is a 1967 Iso Grifo GL, serial number 121, with a completely redesigned body, now by Carrozzeria Bertone. The 327 ci small-block was still under the hood mounted to the center of the car. Winston Goodfellow

Interior of the Iso Grifo GL was completely Italian in styling with wooden dashboard inserts and a large speedometer and tachometer. The steering wheel was by Nardi with the classic wooden rim and aluminum spokes. This car is equipped with a four-speed manual transmission. Winston Goodfellow

The Iso Grifo GL's 327 ci Corvette engine with single four-barrel carburetor. Iso's standard tune helped the 327 pump out 350 hp. Winston Goodfellow

Two Bizzarrini Stradas were built with targa-style roofs and called the Spyder SI, which stood for Stile Italia, the carrozzeria that penned the Spyder design. Alongside the Strada, Bizzarrini also constructed a GT American model, which also featured the 327 ci small-block but used a full independent rear suspension system versus the standard de Dion tube and a fiberglass body. Winston Goodfellow

Bizzarrini's version of the Grifo became known as the Strada, and still housed a 327 ci small-block under the hood. This 1968 Strada's engine produced 350 hp and was mated to a four-speed manual transmission. The Stradas were built 1965-1968, when the company went into receivership and closed in 1969. Winston Goodfellow

The Seventies:
The Emissions Era

"They vacillated so much on this 305 V-8 engine, Joe [Bertsch] and I sat down and put together this program and launched it on our own—and it just got accepted." *Denny Davis*

If the fifties and the sixties can be seen as revolutionary for the Chevrolet small-block V-8, then the seventies must be seen as evolutionary. For Chevrolet, it was evolution under duress. Environmental Protection Agency (EPA) regulations for vehicle emissions and, later, fuel economy caused a complete shift from market-driven performance desires to government-mandated regulations. Power output levels dropped significantly, and no car company was exempt. The research and development that once went into achieving more horsepower per cubic inch now went into reduced pollutants in grams per mile and increased miles per gallon of gasoline to meet the Corporate Average Fuel Economy, or CAFE standards.

With the early efforts to meet these increasingly stringent standards for reducing pollutants, increasing mileage and maintaining good power output were mutually exclusive. The seventies were spent trying to reconcile these seemingly conflicting requirements. Technology had to be advanced greatly in order to do so. The age of the black box under the hood was not far away.

It was during the 1970 model year that Chevrolet introduced the largest small-block ever built by the division: the 400-ci V-8. In some respects, it was an "impossible" engine, forcing a complete rethinking of how V-8 engines are designed for casting and operation coolant flow. How and why the 400 reached production is one of the more intriguing stories in the small-block's long history.

Beginning in 1970, the Corvette was offered with a special solid-lifter LT-1 350 ci small-block that produced 330 hp. This 1971 LT-1 Corvette was the second year the engine was available, but it would go out of production by 1972. These were the signs of the times, as new, stricter federal emissions controls were choking back some of the small-block's power. Jerry Heasley

The 400: A Political Animal

For most of the small-block's history, it had been relatively free of any intra-corporate politics. The engines were conceived and designed based strictly on market demands. The small-block had grown to 350-ci and, realistically, there was no more room to grow. In a product lineup sense, there was really no more *need* to grow, as the big-block 396 and 427 picked up the requirement for further power in the late sixties.

In 1961, Simon E. "Bunky" Knudsen became general manager of Chevrolet while Ed Cole moved up to group vice-president and General Motors director. Knudsen was a strong believer in big-block power and sought to promote it. He was enthusiastic about the introduction of the 409 V-8 in 1962 and was solidly behind the 396 V-8 that came out in 1965 and the 427 V-8 that was released for 1966. Ed Cole, on the other hand, considered the big-block V-8s too heavy and felt the small-block could be enlarged to meet the needs of greater displacement. It was clear to some at Chevrolet that Cole's desire for an even bigger small-block was not based entirely on pragmatism, but also on a fundamental difference in viewpoint between Cole and Knudsen. One of those people believing this was Dick Keinath.

"I'll just give you one word: politics," Keinath said, explaining how the 400 V-8 came about. "The 400 was a very political animal. I think it all boiled down to a feud between Mr. Knudsen and Mr. Cole. The large-block work was all done when Mr. Knudsen was general manager. Mr. Cole never liked the big-block because his engine was the small-block. He was not impressed with big-block engines. So, he realized that there was a need to keep the large-block displacement around, but he thought he could do it by using his small-block as the basis for it. And that's the politics of it."

The idea of expanding the small-block even further was not exactly greeted with enthusiasm by the engineers in the V-8 group. Enlarging the bores to 4.125 in. and lengthening the stroke to 3.75 in. created a host of design challenges. Bill Polkinghorne was design leader of the 400 V-8 project and staff engineer of the V-8 group. Working under

As the air-cleaner decal stated, "Prescribed Power" was what Berger offered. The Berger 1973 Z/28 Camaro was based on the Turbo-Fire 350 ci small-block. Jerry Heasley

Interior appointments of the 1973 Berger Z/28 Camaro followed the stock Z/28. Jerry Heasley

Polkinghorne was Joe Bertsch, who was assistant staff engineer in the V-8 group at the time.

"The Mk IV big-block engines were very expensive and heavy," Bertsch said of Cole's aversion to the big-block. "As I remember, there was a 150-pound weight differential between the small-block V-8 and the Mk IV. The 400 was just an effort to get the maximum displacement possible out of the small-block V-8. The engine had to have the bores siamesed and you couldn't make the bores any larger because, with a 4⅛-inch bore, that only left, as I remember, .28 inch between the cylinders, a very minimal dimension to seal the head gaskets at that point."

In the 350 V-8 and previous engines, coolant was able to circulate around the cylinder bores. Enlarging the bores by .125 in. required blending these cylinder bores, or "siameseing" the bores while still allowing for sufficient cylinder bore wall thickness. This completely did away with coolant circulating around the bores, and Chevrolet engineers endeavoured to solve this problem by drilling steam holes in the deck of the engine block to prevent steam pockets from building up and causing cooling problems. There were six of these holes per cylinder bank. Enlarging the bores also created another problem.

"One of the problems was oil consumption," Bertsch said. "This wasn't particularly related to the siamesed bores. It was related to the fact that the bores had been opened up without moving the head bolts. The distance between the bore wall and the head bolts was [roughly] .06 inch less. What happened, then, when you put the head bolts in and torqued them up, it caused the bores near the head bolt boss to bulge. You could look at the engines after they had run and see the shiny pattern in the bores right at the head bolt bosses where the rings lost contact with the bore. There wasn't anything we could do to fix it. Typically, we had 400s that ran in the 700 miles-per-quart range. At that time, the yardstick for what was satisfactory oil economy was 1,000 miles per quart.

"One of the other potential problems that I was concerned about on the engine—and this was directly related to the siamesed bores—was during laboratory testing, the engine showed a tendency to preignite. The siamesed bore section ran considerably hotter than the water-cooled portion of the bore. Under

Berger Chevrolet entered the market with its own line of limited-production modified muscle cars in the fashion of Don Yenko and Baldwin Motion. This was Berger's 1973 Z/28. Jerry Heasley

conditions where the spark advance was over-advanced, it would have a tendency to blow holes in the ring land in the area adjacent to the siamesed bore. This only showed up in laboratory tests, not in the field during customer service. To minimize this possibility, we restricted application to cars and light-duty trucks."

The new 350 ci Turbo-Fire of the 1970 Z/28. Only 8,733 Z/28s were built in 1970 as the Trans-Am phenomenon was winding down to its dying days when the corporations would exit from the race. Musclecar Review

Rear view of the 1970 Camaro Z/28 with the new 350 ci small-block called for by the SCCA's Trans-Am rulebook. In this form, the Turbo-Fire produced some 330 hp. The Z/28 package also included dual exhausts and power brakes. Musclecar Review

The 400-ci V-8 was the first small-block to be equipped with four-bolt main bearing caps at the time of its introduction. This was not a decision for high-performance applications, but one based on the use of the nodular iron crankshaft. The decision to go with a nodular iron crankshaft was based on cost compared to a forged iron crankshaft, and the four-bolt main bearing caps were insurance to give this crankshaft greater support.

"That was a carry-over of the design practice of the 350 V-8," Bertsch said of the decision to use a nodular iron crankshaft in the 400 V-8. "As I remember, the 350 truck engine and the high-compression 350 had four-bolt mains. Putting four-bolt mains on the 400 was pretty much a carry-over of that practice. The four-bolt mains were primarily a fix introduced on the engines not particularly to cure bulkhead cracking, [but] it was primarily put on the engine to increase crankshaft durability during the development of the nodular iron crankshaft. The reason was cost. At that point, that was worth between five and six dollars in cost savings per crank. Four-bolt mains did not exist before the nodular iron cranks.

"In 1967," Bertsch continued, "the first year of the 350, it came out with forged crankshaft and two-bolt mains. That was a carry-over from what had existed on the 327. The nodular iron crankshaft was introduced in 1968, and that's when the four-bolt mains came into effect, primarily to provide more rigidity in the crankcase to limit the amount of deflections and stress of the nodular iron crankshaft."

As an extra measure of insurance, the decision was made to increase main bearing diameter to 2.65 in., while the rod journal diameter remained at 2.10 in. The fact was, there was no room to make the rod journal diameter any larger. The connecting rod center-to-center distance was shorter than the standard rod heretofore used—5.565 in. for the 400 V-8 compared to the standard 5.700-in. rod.

"The stroke of the engine was limited by the clearance of the camshaft by the connecting rod," Bertsch explained. "In order to even achieve the stroke of 3.75 inches on the 400, the guys had to cut down the bolt boss height on the connecting rod to clear the cam. That produced what I considered a considerably weaker rod. That was a concern on the engine from the standpoint of high-speed operation. It was not as strong as the 350 rod because of the way the bolt boss was cut down. It made the section thinner between the connecting rod bore and the outside surface of the bolt boss."

Knowing this, Chevrolet chose not only to restrict the engine to cars and light-duty trucks, but the engine would only be offered with an automatic transmission.

"The primary reason for limiting the engine with only the automatic transmission was my concern for the durability of the rod," explained Bertsch. "Lab tests indicated that the 400 rod was a lot weaker than the standard 350 rod. So I did not want to release the engine in any applications that would have high-speed operation. We released it with automatics where the highest speed would be limited to the shift speed of the transmissions. If we put it in manuals, there'd be no limit—the guy could red-line it. As it turned out, we never had problems with the rod in actual customer service."

When Knudsen left Chevrolet in 1968 after the 400 V-8 engine project was underway, some interpreted this as political fallout. Knudsen, however, had been offered the presidency of Ford Motor Company, an offer few automotive executives would have turned down. E. M. "Pete" Estes took over as general manager of Chevrolet. His tenure in that position at the division was short, as John Z. DeLorean took over in 1970 after the introduction of the 1970 models, including the new 400 V-8.

The largest displacement small-block was offered as optional equipment in two power levels that year: the two-barrel version with a 9.0:1 cr designed to run on regular gas, rated at 265 hp having the RPO LF6; and the four-barrel version rated at 330 hp with its RPO order code LS3.

In the full-size Chevrolet, the two-barrel 250-hp 350 V-8 was made the standard V-8. Optional small-block V-8s included the L-48 300-hp four-barrel 350, or the two-barrel 265-hp 400. In the new Monte Carlo, the same standard and optional engines were offered, with an

Next page
Don Yenko owned a Chevrolet dealership in Canonsburg, Pennsylvania, where he specialized in muscle car sales. He was pleased with the Chevrolet muscle but always believed that more was better, so in 1965 he set up Yenko Sports Cars to modify Chevrolet Camaros, Chevelles, Corvettes and odd Novas. This 1970 Yenko Deuce Nova LT-1 inherited the 350 ci, 370 hp small-block from the Corvette line under Yenko's hand. This rare car is now in the Otis Chandler Collection. Jerry Heasley

The 350 ci V-8 is the longest-running member of the small-block family, reaching the quarter-century mark in 1992. It is a great powerplant for street enthusiasts today. This 300 hp Turbo-Fire 350 ci V-8 is from 1970. Chevrolet

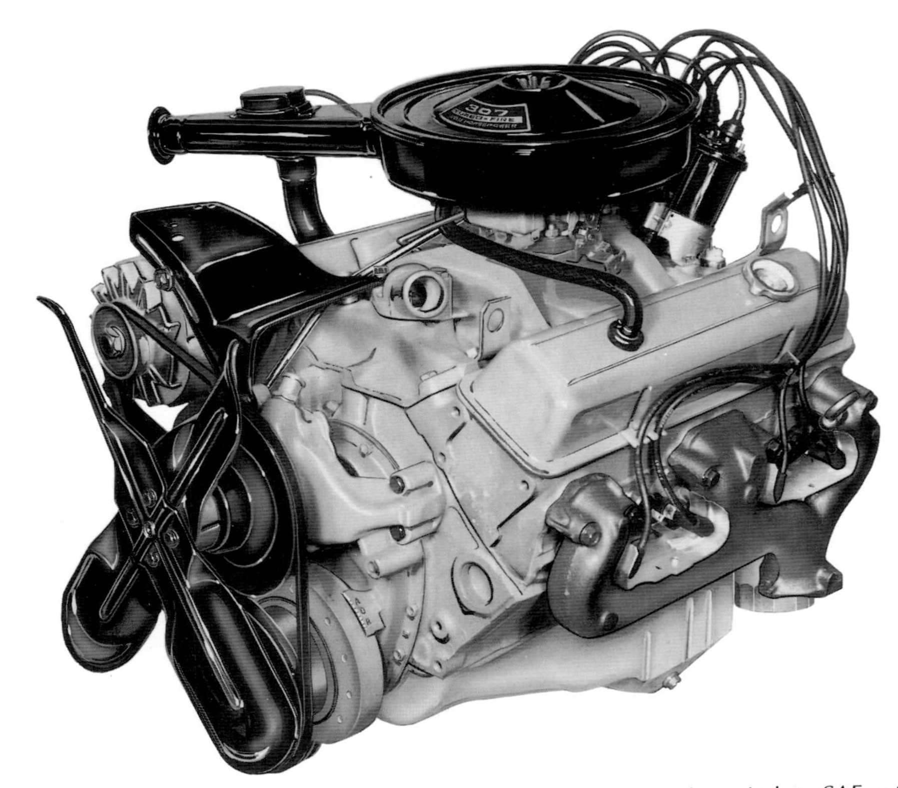

The 307 ci V-8 was the base V-8 engine for Chevelles, Novas and Camaros in the early 1970s. For most of its production life, the 2 bbl 307 was rated at 200 hp. A drop in compression ratios and a switch to SAE net horsepower lowered this to 115 hp by 1973. Chevrolet

350

carburetor had 245 gross bhp at 4800 rpm, while the engine was rated at 255 hp in the Caprice and station wagons. Oddly, the optional 400 V-8 was also rated at 255 hp.

The standard V-8 in the 1971 Monte Carlo was the 245-hp 350 V-8. The only optional small-block was the 270-hp four-barrel 350 V-8.

In the Camaro that year, the 200-hp 307 was still the base V-8. Aside from the aforementioned Z-28, there was the optional two-barrel 245-hp 350 V-8, or the 270-hp 350 V-8 as part of the SS350 package.

In place of the base 307 V-8 in the Nova, you could order the two-barrel 245-hp 350 V-8 or the SS350 package with the 270-hp 350 V-8. These two optional small-block V-8s were also available in the Chevelle.

Chevrolet's performance flagship, the Corvette, came standard with the 8.5:1 cr, 270-hp 350 V-8. The only optional small-block was the 350-hp LT-1.

In 1972, all manufacturers fully adopted the S.A.E. net horsepower rating that reflected engine output as installed in the car. This lowered the numbers even further. Enthusiast magazines and their readers bemoaned the rapid decline in performance, but the situation was due to get worse. Chevrolet engineers struggled to maintain decent performance while meeting emissions levels that were scheduled to become increasingly more stringent.

As an example of the new net rating, the base 350 V-8 in the Corvette was rated at 200 hp. The LT-1 was now rated at 255 hp. There was a rare factory option, the ZR-1, which was a special 350 V-8 at a cost of $1,010.01. According to the *Standard Catalog of Chevrolet, 1912-1990*, only thirty Corvettes with the ZR-1 option were built.

Just how bad was the drop in small-block performance in 1972? *Motor Trend* did a comparison test of the Z-28 and the Datsun 240Z for the August 1972 issue. The LT-1 (in its last year of production) Z-28, equipped with a four-speed manual transmission and 3.73:1 rear end, reached 60 mph in 7.7 seconds and covered the quarter-mile in 15.2 seconds at 86.6 mph.

Chevrolet, and every other manufacturer, was looking at the decline in the performance market that was directly proportional to the decline in performance itself. Not only were more stringent emissions standards on the horizon, but Congress was making noises about proposing fuel economy standards as well. The funds that once went into performance and performance parts development shifted to emissions and fuel economy. Chevrolet was looking into developing a new generation of reduced-displacement small-block V-8s to meet these new realities. It looked like performance at Chevrolet was on the ropes and going down for the count, but an interesting thing happened. With the decline in street performance came a corresponding rise of enthusiast interest in sanctioned racing.

"Chevrolet built this tremendous image of performance almost exclusively in the seventies when there was nothing going on with production cars," said Howell. "The performance image went off the street and onto drag racing and circle track. Chevrolet captured that market by having economical-to-buy and readily-available parts. Also, during the sixties and seventies, we perfected back-door racing policies to where we would maximize our effort in the field and maximize Chevrolet's image, even though the corporation wouldn't advertise the [racing] success.

"There's a negative advertising involved there that most people don't realize," Howell continued. "If you win the race, nobody else can advertise, you're taking away the ability for other people to crow about their accomplishments. In a negative advertising sense, Chevrolet dominated an awful lot of the performance world in that period.

"During that time period, we recognized that grassroots racing was our salvation as a performance image. We started preserving our good high-performance parts from the sixties. In February 1963, the corporation cracked down on racing by Chevrolet and Pontiac. Pontiac eventually cut everything from its product line that had to do with performance. They quit making forged crankshafts, forged connecting rods, forged pistons—the good parts—and in four years they were nowhere.

"When Chevrolet pulled their horns back in," said Howell, "they said, 'Well, we better keep the forged crankshafts because we need them for trucks. We'll keep the premium forged connecting rods—they cost us fifty cents more

Team mechanics work on a McLaren small-block during a break in 1960s Can Am action. The team small-blocks typically produced about 465 hp and with the cast-iron block, provided exceptional reliability. With the arrival of the McLaren M-8, the team switched over to Chevrolet ZL-1 big-blocks, bored and stroked to 494 ci and producing upward of 740 hp. David Gooley

but . . .' There were a lot of people at Chevrolet who were latent racers and every time they could save a good part from the hangman, they did it. These were all production parts. You went into your Chevy dealer and bought them. We always kept them in the parts book and people could always go to a dealership and buy them. The car magazines picked up on this. That's where everyone else got behind because it was going on under everyone's nose. It was right out in the open. You could buy all these parts from Chevrolet and nobody else was putting two and two together and realized what it was doing for the image."

Thanks to the foresight of those enthusiasts at Chevrolet, many of the high performance parts and engines developed during the sixties are still available today, and are augmented by new

Iso of Italy continued car construction into the 1970s and had some of its greatest sales successes in the United States and Europe during this decade. This 1970 Iso Grifo, serial number 331, was the last of the Series I Grifos with open headlamps. Power still came from the 327 ci small-block producing some 350 hp in Iso tuning. Winston Goodfellow

ones being developed. In the early seventies, however, Chevrolet and other car companies were under seige. Ways had to be found to meet the forthcoming fuel economy standards and emissions levels. One of the ways Chevrolet felt it could do that was looking for new ways to meet these standards, and another was by offering reduced displacement V-8s.

The End of Performance?

Ever since the small-block V-8 had been introduced, performance had sold cars. These new government standards were certainly sapping performance and it appeared things would get worse. The future of performance at Chevrolet looked bleak.

"There was a time when they thought the Corvette would never make it," Louis Cuttitta admitted. "They'd say, 'We're going to have to delete the Corvette. We're not going to be able to sell it.' I remember very well Dave McClellan saying to me, 'Lou, you've got to do something.' The pressure was on us because management wanted the Corvette to market. And, for myself, how could I afford to be responsible for getting people laid off at the Corvette plant? Those things weighed on my mind. How were we going to meet these emissions requirements?

"One of the things we had to do was change some of the priorities. Corvettes notoriously had a steep axle, meaning an axle pushing 3.74 instead of 2.56. A 3.74 axle gives you a lot of performance off the line, the other axle not quite so much. Right off the bat we learned if you cut back on performance, we could give you fuel economy and the emissions would be lower because the throughput through the exhaust system is lower. In other words, if you only have to turn the engine 2000 rpms instead of 3500 rpms, you're not going to put out as many pollutants. So, one of the key things was to change the axle ratio in the Corvette. Then, there was a time we didn't have a manual transmission.

"We had to change the air cleaner a little bit to improve the way the air entered the carburetor because that would generate hydrocarbons on deceleration. The car had to run on 91 octane with no detonation at a given humidity and a given temperature, and we had to lower the NOx (oxides of nitrogen) emissions. Well, the way to do that was lower the compression ratio. Now, nobody wanted to do that, particularly in the Corvette, but we did. By lowering the compression ratio, which gave us better hydrocarbon control and better NOx control, it hurt fuel economy and performance, but it meant we could sell the car. On that basis, they bought.

"We really wrestled with emission all through the seventies and I think that whole period—the seventies—General Motors didn't go anywhere. It seemed to me like we were in the doldrums.

"The only thing exciting that happened in the seventies was Ed Cole put together a team of people that he thought were the outstanding people at General Motors to plan for the late seventies and early eighties emissions systems. There were 134 of us from the whole corporation. I was fortunate enough to be one of them. Bob Price, Jim Spaulding, George Ford, Sam Cataldo, Larry Weathers, Dick Keinath, Jack Layton, Don McPherson, Al Rasegan, Bob Wiltse, Pete Estes, John Delorean, Bob Stemple, Al Kolbe, Mr. Zimmer, Howard Carol, Ray Nicholson, John Moles, Duane Tangee—these were just a few."

This brain trust was responsible for formulating the direction of research and development regarding fuel economy and emissions for the future as well as offering products vehicle buyers truly wanted. Steps in this direction had already been taken, and one path for those at Chevrolet was to offer reduced displacements of the small-block V-8 as a means of boosting fuel economy.

The 370 hp 350 ci LT-1 V-8 was introduced in 1970 as an option in the Corvette. This engine was standard in the Z/28 that year but with a 365 hp rating. It featured an 11:1 compression ratio, forged pistons, connecting rods and crankshaft, four-bolt main bearing caps and solid-lifter camshaft. It ranks among the most desirable small-block V-8s Chevrolet ever offered. Chevrolet

The 262-ci V-8

The first of these reduced displacement V-8s was the 262-ci V-8 introduced in select 1975 Chevrolet models. It had a bore of 3.671 in. and a stroke of 3.10 in., making it the smallest V-8 Chevrolet had ever built since the small-block's introduction. Intake valve diameter was 1.72 in. and exhaust valve diameter was 1.30 in. Although it had 2.45 in. diameter main journals and 2.10 in. rod journals, the crankshaft, with its 3.10 stroke, was unique to this engine. The crankshaft was nodular iron and was secured using two-bolt main bearing caps. The compression ratio was 8.5:1. The engine was fed by a two-barrel Rochester carburetor. The engine that year was rated at 110 hp at 3600 rpm. (Note: the 262-ci V-8 was not offered for sale in California. In its place was offered the 350-ci V-8 with four-barrel carburetor, rated at 155 hp at 3800 rpm.)

Chevrolet's first attempt to offer a reduced displacement V-8 to meet the demands of the seventies was less than an overwhelming success. The engine proved problematic from the very start. It consumed more development time than expected, and this was attributable to its oversquare bore-to-stroke ratio. When the bore is larger than the stroke, the bore/stroke ratio is greater than 1.0 and the engine is oversquare. If the bore and stroke are equal, the bore/stroke ratio is 1.0 and the engine is considered square. If the bore is less than the stroke, the bore/stroke ratio is less than 1.0 and the engine is undersquare.

"The project got started because at that time we were interested in downsizing engines to achieve better fuel economy," recalled Bertsch. "The bore and stroke was very oversquare. What is wrong with an oversquare engine from an efficiency standpoint? The burn rate of the combustion chamber is too slow. The smaller you make the cylinder, the shorter the burn path becomes. It's more desirable from a standpoint to increase the burn rate of the engine to make the cylinders smaller. What happens when you go overboard with that is, you start to grossly restrict the size of the valves you can put in the engine, so the horsepower of the engine goes down. You trade off one attribute for another.

"There is no way to calculate the optimum bore-to-stroke ratio. It's a matter of making a judgement—how do I want to balance the horsepower of the engine with the valve sizes against the engine's efficiency? What you find when you do surveys of what other designers have previously done is the preponderance of engines built in the world fall within that .95 to 1.05 bore-to-stroke range. The ratio on the 262 V-8 was up around 1.25. What the oversquare bore/stroke ratio required you to do was retard the spark too much. You actually killed the efficiency of the engine to get emission control by retarding the spark, and as a result of that, you lost fuel economy. With the advent of emission laws it became necessary to limit the emission of hydrocarbons and CO in the exhaust.

Hydrocarbons were basically controlled by retarding the spark on the engine from its optimum values. Retarding the spark increased the exhaust gas temperature so that more postoxidation of the unburned hydrocarbons would take place in the hotter exhaust gas stream in the exhaust manifold. Unfortunately, retarding the spark also decreased the engine efficiency, and in the early seventies significant losses in fuel economy were accepted in order to meet the hydrocarbon emission standard.

"The 262 required so much spark retard when calibrated for 91 octane fuel, due to its slow burn rate, that its fuel economy was lousy. I know from the people that were working on the emissions and fuel calibration of the engine that they were really P.O.'d about the whole affair. Everybody complained about it from a performance standpoint and a fuel economy standpoint. But that unsatisfactory experience on that engine led us to revise all our ideas about getting these other engines we were going to downsize in the future to be a more square bore-to-stroke ratio. We came to the conclusion we had certainly made the wrong decision in going so much oversquare with the 262.

"This experience on the 262 led us to a better acceptance of the engineering staff position on the effect of bore/stroke ratio on the hydrocarbon emission of the engine and resulted in setting up ratios for the 305 and [later the] 267 which were more nearly square, these being 1.07 and 1.00 respectively."

The push was on in the 1970s to meet current and future emission standards for cars. High Energy Ignition (HEI) and the catalytic converter introduced in 1975 were just two of the means employed to meet the standards. This Monte Carlo chassis was designed to meet the standards. The cutaway catalytic converter is visible. Chevrolet

The 305-ci V-8

The lessons learned from the 262-ci V-8 were immediately applied to another engine that followed the 262 by about a year. That engine was the 305-ci V-8, introduced in 1976. This engine had the same 3.48 in. stroke of the 350-ci V-8, coupled with a 3.74 in. bore. This permitted increasing intake valve diameter to 1.84 in. and exhaust valve diameter to 1.50 in. The crankshaft was the same one used in the 350 V-8. When introduced in 1976, the compression ratio was 8.5:1 and horsepower was 140 at 3800 rpm with 245 lb-ft of torque at 2000 rpm. The 305 became the new base V-8 engine in small and mid-size Chevrolet models, supplanting the 350 V-8.

"When we got the direction for a 300 cubic-inch engine again," Bertsch said, "instead of reintroducing the 307, which had a 3⅞ inch bore by a 3¼ inch stroke, we decided to retain the crankshaft stroke of the 350 and debore the engine to make it more nearly square—and that engine has been a tremendous success."

Why didn't Chevrolet simply reintroduce the 307-ci V-8? While the 307 was a good torque engine based on its oversquare design having a bore/stroke ratio of 1.19, it was a poor engine in terms of fuel economy and exhaust emissions. The new small-block V-8 had to have a more favorable bore/stroke ratio to satisfy these new requirements. What was done, essentially, was to debore the 350-ci V-8. The design of the 305-ci V-8 was driven by the need for a new base V-8 engine that met toughening emission standards and achieved good fuel economy.

"The GM Advanced Engineering Group was developing data and theories on the factors affecting the level of unburned hydrocarbons," Bertsch said of the emissions research conducted in the early seventies. "These factors were the internal surface area of the combustion chamber and the internal crevice volume in the combustion chamber. In the case of the area, the theory was that during combustion, the flame would quench out and incompletely burn in a small boundary layer adjacent to the internal surfaces and be expelled as unburned hydrocarbons during the exhaust stroke.

"Similarly," Bertsch continued, "unburned mixture would be compressed into the crevice volumes where the temperature would be too low for the mixture to burn during the power stroke and would re-expand and exhaust unburned during the exhaust stroke. The bore/stroke ratio affected both the internal surface area and the crevice volumes. The primary crevice volume was the top ring land clearance and the head gasket setback, both of which would obviously become smaller with a smaller bore diameter. The internal surface area of the combustion chamber would become smaller with a smaller-diameter, deeper chamber."

Proof of the 305-ci V-8's success is the fact that it is still in production. But getting the 305-ci V-8 *approved* for production was not an easy matter, perhaps because of the bad experience the division had had developing the 262-ci V-8. Denny Davis worked in the V-8 basic engine group under Joe Bertsch at the time a new, reduced-displacement V-8 was being proposed. He had, by then, put in nearly a quarter of a century with the Chevrolet Division.

Davis started work right out of high school, when he was eighteen years old, in the detail drafting department of the General Motors Institute in 1949. During the next four years, he also worked in the test labs and the Milford Proving Grounds. He graduated from GMI in August 1953 and joined the engine drafting group as a design draftsman.

"In 1957, I was assigned to the Corvair engine design team," Davis said, taking over his story. "In '58, I was assigned to the test lab for the Corvair. In 1959, I joined Zora Arkus-Duntov's high-performance group. There was an opening in the group because Dick Keinath was going to the production group with the aluminum cylinder head. Dick had been working on the aluminum cylinder head for the small-block engine. It was considered a possibility as a production package and Dick elected to go from Duntov's group to the production engine group to maintain control of that cylinder head because he was very involved with it. That left an opening in Zora's group. I was interviewed for the job, was accepted and took the job with Zora. I stayed until 1967 when the group was disbanded, then spent ten months working in the transmission group.

"In 1968, I was reassigned as a one-man Corvette engine group with the task of designing the cooling package to allow the use of air conditioning on the Mk IV engine in the Corvette. In 1969, I was transferred to the basic engine group."

Davis remained in the basic V-8 engine design group during the seventies, becoming overall supervisor in 1978, when Joe Bertsch was promoted to the advanced engine design group. In 1982, Davis himself began working in the advanced engine design group. In January 1985, he became manager of the 2.8 liter V-6 lab development group. He retired in 1987 with nearly forty years working for Chevrolet.

Davis worked closely with Joe Bertsch on the 305 V-8 engine project and he had his own unique perspective on how the engine project got started.

Iso also produced a limited number of Grifo Targa cars. This car, serial number 314, has a 327 ci small-block with 300 hp through a five-speed ZF gearbox. Winston Goodfellow

Previous page
The svelte lines of the Iso Grifo make it one of the most beautiful of Italian exotic cars, and with power from the Chevrolet small-block, one of the easiest to own in the United States. In the early 1990s, a prototype Grifo 90 has been unveiled—still using the small-block as the powerplant. Winston Goodfellow

"We were told to come up with a five-liter engine," Davis said. "I had decided that the thing to do was combine a 3.75 bore with a 3.48 stroke that gave us something close to five liters. We recognized at the time we were talking engines that were felt to be better from an emissions standpoint because of crevice volume, that it should be closer to square—have more stroke and less bore.

"Joe Bertsch was the supervisor of the V-8 group when I was in there," he said. "They vacillated so much on this 305 V-8 engine, Joe and I sat down and put together this program and launched it on our own—and it just got accepted. As I recall, it ultimately had to go to Don McPherson, who was chief engineer at that time. It was one of those things when someone looked at it and saw it in

Beginning in mid-1970, Iso introduced its Series II Grifo with a longer nose and half-covered headlamps. This car, serial number 298, has a 327 ci small-block producing 350 hp with a five-speed ZF gearbox. This car has the deep-finned Iso aluminum oil pan. Winston Goodfellow

place, they just didn't argue and made the decision to go with it."

The 305 ci V-8 replaced the 262 V-8 in 1976 as the base V-8. Bore was 3.74 in. and stroke was 3.48 in. With a more favorable bore/stroke ratio, emissions and fuel economy were improved over the 262 V-8. RPO engine code was LG4. Chevrolet

Performance in the Late Seventies

What kind of performance did the family of small-block V-8s have in the late seventies? Besides all the other engine modifications that had to be done to meet emissions standards, there was a new, costly fly in the ointment—the catalytic converter. This effectively did away with dual exhaust systems and made the single exhaust systems more restrictive. On the positive side, the catalytic converter permitted recalibration of the carburetor and ignition timing to boost fuel economy lost during the previous years. The catalytic converter required unleaded gasoline, and the petroleum companies had been working for several years to reduce the amount of lead in gasoline. This, too, had a positive effect on the environment. It must not be forgotten why all this emissions work was being done: to make the air we breathe cleaner, or at least get no worse than it was.

It was Ed Cole, in fact, who had put pressure on the petroleum industry to eliminate lead from gasoline to permit lower compression ratios and catalytic converters necessary to meet emissions standards.

However, this was not a paramount concern to buyers of cars having to deal with sticker shock and the very real drop in performance from only five years before. Cars were heavier due to front and rear five-mph bumpers and side-impact door guards as a result of additional government regulations. For the small-block enthusiast, this was not the best of times.

When the 262-ci V-8 was introduced in 1975, it was available in the new Monza and the Nova. However, this engine could not meet California's stiff emissions regulations. In a February 18, 1975, news release, Chevrolet announced that in place of the 262-ci V-8, a two-barrel, 350-ci V-8 with three-speed automatic transmission and 2.29:1 rear axle ratio would be offered in these cars sold in that state. *Road & Track* tested a 1975 Monza 2 + 2 with the 262-ci V-8. Despite its diminutive size, it was no lightweight. Curb weight was 3,200 lb. Equipped with an automatic transmission and economy 2.93:1 rear axle, the Monza accelerated to 60 mph in 13.4 seconds and covered the quarter-mile in 19.5 seconds doing just over 72 mph. Top speed was 103 mph. Average fuel economy was seventeen miles per gallon.

In 1976 *Road & Track* tested a Camaro Type LT with the 4-bbl 350 V-8 with automatic transmission and 3.08:1 rear axle ratio. Curb weight was now over 4,000 pounds. The editors wrote, "Our acceleration testing made it clear that emission controls have taken much of the zip out of the Camaro as we managed a 0-60 mph time of 10.1 seconds compared to 8.8 sec for a 1970 version of the car with the 350 V-8. But, as we said earlier, performance is no longer the name of the game. In terms of driveability, the 350 V-8 proved to be as smooth as we could ask with no signs of lean surge, stumbling or cold or hot starting problems. It's long been evident that American manufacturers have the answers when it comes to building V-8 engines with useful torque and ample performance and the Camaro carries that tradition forward despite retarded ignition timing, air pumps, catalytic converters, and so on."

With the dramatic impact emission controls had on small-block performance, Chevrolet felt it could not, in all good conscience, offer the Camaro Z-28, so the model was dropped after the 1974 model year. That didn't mean Chevrolet's most famous Camaro was gone forever, however. The engineers at 30007 Van Dyke in Warren had every intention of bringing the car back, but more work had to be done to return the 350 V-8 to a level of performance worthy of the Z-28 badge.

Emission controls took their toll on the small-block V-8 in the later 1970s. The 262-ci V-8 was dropped from the product line after only one year of production and replaced by the 305-ci V-8 in 1976. In 1977, the 400-ci V-8 was dropped from the

The last of the Iso Grifo Targas was this car, serial number 353, one of only four Series II Targas. In the early 1970s, Iso switched to the 7 liter Chevrolet big-block for power in the Grifo series and eventually went to the Ford 351 Cleveland in 1972. Alongside the Grifo, Iso produced the four-door limousine S4 Fidia and the two-door sports sedan Lele and Lele S. The factory closed its doors in 1974. Winston Goodfellow

passenger car line, but continued in vans and trucks for several more years.

In a move that surprised many Chevy fans, the Camaro Z-28 was reintroduced as a mid-year model in 1977. A great deal of work had gone into making the new Z-28 an excellent all-around performer, not a straight-line screamer. Chevrolet was still having difficulty making the 350 V-8 meet both the expectations of the enthusiast and the demands of the EPA. *Car & Driver* put the Z-28 in a head-to-head competition with the Pontiac Trans-Am. The Z-28 reached 60 mph in 8.6 seconds and covered the quarter-mile in 16.3 seconds at 83.1 mph. Much better times, literally, were coming for the Z-28 in the eighties.

Work had been progressing on finally putting a four-barrel carburetor on the 305-ci V-8, but that had not been the original plan for the engine.

"The 305 was only to be a two-barrel engine," Davis said. "I was constantly working to run it off as a four-barrel. I got caught a couple of times [and was told], 'Davis, get that off the dynamometer. It's not supposed to be there. I told you not to do that.' We finally snuck a run through on our own—clandestinely. It did have probably less power loss due to borderline spark advance than virtually any other of our V-8 configurations. It was attributed to our bore/stroke combination being more square. Ultimately, it was found out that it was the configuration we were running because later engines were much more sensitive to spark advance."

The four-barrel, 305-ci V-8 finally did appear in 1979. With an 8.4:1 compression ratio, the 4-bbl 305-ci V-8 was rated at 160 hp at 4000 rpm with 235 lb-ft of torque at 2400 rpm. The two-barrel 305 with the same compression ratio was rated at 130 hp at 3200 rpm with 245 lb-ft of torque at 2000 rpm.

The 350-ci V-8 was available in two slightly different versions in 1979, both with four-barrel carburetors. The first was optional in the Malibu Wagon, Nova, Impala and Caprice, having an 8.2:1 compression ratio, rated at 165-170 hp at 3800 rpm with 260-270 lb-ft of torque at 2400 rpm. The other 350 V-8 was optional in the Camaro and standard in the Z-28, and was rated at 175 hp at 4000 rpm with 270 lb-ft of torque at 2400 rpm. It appears this was simply a numbers game because the horsepower level of the Z-28 engine was taken at a higher rpm where the power would naturally be higher; the torque was virtually the same for both engines.

The base 350 V-8 in the Corvette for 1979, the L48, was being rated at 195 hp at 4000 rpm with 285 lb-ft of torque at 3200 rpm running a 8.2:1 compression ratio. The optional L-82, with an 8.9:1 cr, was rated at 225 hp at 5200 rpm with 270 lb-ft torque at 3600 rpm.

Chevrolet continued its efforts to increase fuel economy and reduce emissions by offering a new small-block V-8 in 1979 with lessons learned from the ill-fated 262-ci V-8 and the 305-ci V-8.

The 267-ci V-8

In 1979, Chevrolet introduced the 267-ci V-8. This engine had a 3.50 in. bore and the familiar 3.48 in. stroke. Essentially, Chevrolet engineers debored the 305-ci V-8. This effectively gave the engine a bore stroke ratio of 1.0. It had the same crankshaft specifications as the 305 and 350 V-8s. Intake and exhaust valve diameters were those used on the 262 V-8: 1.72 in. diameter intake valves and 1.38 in. diameter exhaust valves. With an 8.2:1 compression ratio and Rochester two-barrel carburetor, this new small-block was rated at 125 hp at 3800 rpm with 215 lb-ft of torque at 2400 rpm. Proof of the engine's cleanliness was its availability in California as well as the other states. The 267-ci V-8 was optional only in the Monte Carlo and the Malibu that year.

In the late 1970s, the LM1 became the top 350 ci V-8 offered in Camaros, but the flashy aluminum valve covers of the early seventies were gone. In 1979, it had a power rating of 175 hp at 400 rpm and 270 lb-ft of torque at 2400 rpm. This LM1 was photographed in 1977. Chevrolet

The 267 V-8 was a far better engine in terms of fuel economy and exhaust emissions than the 262 V-8, surviving into the early eighties. However, Chevrolet had been working diligently on V-6 engines and these would eventually alleviate the need for a small-displacement V-8 in the Chevrolet lineup.

The seventies had been a difficult, indeed traumatic, period for Chevrolet Engineering. The limits of emission control using carburetors were approaching and Chevrolet looked to new technologies in the areas of induction and engine controls to meet future emissions levels and restore long-lost power and performance to the small-block V-8.

RADAR WARNING RECEIVER
ESCORT
RADAR WARNING RECEIVER

Mobil 1

MED

brembo
GOTTI
RONAL

MORRISON

PRO

The Eighties:
The Return of Performance

"We weren't trying to create a race engine, although we did have somebody run one at the 24 Hours of Daytona in 1990 and finish seventh in the GTO class in the race, which I think is pretty amazing."

Jim Covey on the 5.7 liter H.O.

During the later seventies when the grand experiment known as the "energy crisis" caused long lines to form at gas stations all across the country, automotive pundits were predicting that the V-8 was doomed. Like dinosaurs facing extinction, it was only a matter of time, some wrote, before the gas-guzzling V-8 would vanish from the face of the earth. Alarmists were wringing their hands saying the world would run out of oil in fifty years, or 100 years, or—well, it really didn't matter. Americans had to end their love affair with the automobile, they stated soberly. Some automotive journalists were caught up in this mindless crusade and did their best to hammer the nail into the V-8's coffin. Even our president said we must tighten our belts and sacrifice.

Corvettes pour around a curve in SCCA race action from 1991. The 350 ci small-block probably reached its highest degree of perfection in the matched Corvettes used in the Corvette Challenge series in 1988-89, and the sophisticated tuning and race setups developed in that series continue to benefit Corvette racers in the 1990s.

As many soon found out, there was no shortage of oil, only a shortage of common sense. There was no energy crisis, simply a crisis of confidence. The Arab oil embargo caused many in industry and government to overreact and interfere with the free flow of oil at market prices. When this happened, long lines formed at gas pumps, even/odd rationing entered American's vocabulary, and prices rose to alarming levels. The prices may have been high by U.S. standards, but they were still low compared to what Britons and Europeans had been paying for years. Cars equipped with big V-8s languished on dealers lots, and smart buyers snapped up some real bargains with the knowledge that gas prices would eventually come down, which they did.

Downsizing became an automotive industry trend. Cars would get smaller, and so would engines. Some enthusiast magazines printed articles saying Camaros and Corvettes of the future would be powered by V-6s. Small-block enthusiasts became alarmed.

Fortunately, cooler heads prevailed at Chevrolet. Yes, V-6 engines were being developed for the future, but they were not going to be the sole V-configuration in Chevrolet automobiles. The product mix would include four-cylinders, V-6s *and* V-8s. The rumors of the small-block V-8's death were greatly exaggerated.

The key to the small-block's survival in the eighties was technology. The two areas where large sums of money for research and development were going to be spent were induction systems and computer controls. Actually, these two areas were interlocking and were developed concurrently. Fuel management, and thus emissions and fuel economy, had to progress by an order of magnitude heretofore unprecedented if Chevrolet was to meet the standards set by government and the demands of its customers.

Throttle Body Injection

The first of these new fuel management systems to be developed was Throttle Body Injection (TBI). Research and development of TBI took place at the Emission Control System Project Center at the GM Proving Grounds in Milford, Michigan. Work was begun in the late seventies on a new means of low-pressure fuel delivery that was controlled electronically, but was less complex and less expensive than the Electronic Fuel Injection (EFI) developed earlier.

Electronic Fuel Injection systems are high-pressure systems operating between 39 and 79 psi, and they required an expensive, precise, high-pressure fuel pump and an in-tank low-pressure boost pump.

"The motivating factor behind the hard work to obtain an acceptable low-pressure fuel system was the elimination of the precision high-pressure fuel pump and its associated cost," wrote Lauren L. Bowler in his S.A.E. paper titled, "Throttle Body Fuel Injection (TBI)—An Integrated Control System."

The primary components of the TBI system are the throttle body unit itself and the Electronic Control Module (ECM), otherwise known as the "blackbox."

Different models of TBI system were planned for a variety of GM powerplants, each of them using variants of the five main components to the TBI unit. The main components are (1) fuel injector, (2) throttle position sensors, (3) Idle Air Control (IAC) valve assembly, (4) fuel meter body assembly and (5) fuel meter cover assembly. The low-pressure fuel injectors were developed by the General Motors' Diesel Equipment Division (which was consolidated with Rochester Products Division in 1981) with an eye on less expensive manufacturing procedures compared to the high-pressure fuel injectors. Rochester Products Division handled the throttle body itself.

The Electronic Control Module was initially developed by the Santa Barbara Operations of GM's Delco Electronics and manufactured at Delco's Milwaukee, Wisconsin, facility. This first-generation ECM included an eight-bit microprocessor with a sampling rate of 500,000 steps per second.

The microprocessor consisted of a General Motors Custom Microcomputer (GMCM) chip set incorporating large-scale integrated (LSI) circuits. These, in turn, included the microprocessing unit (MPU), power control unit (PCU), engine control unit (ECU), and an eight-channel analog-to-digital converter of sensor signals for manifold absolute pressure (MAP), throttle position, coolant temperature, mixture temperature and barometer. Finally, there were memory chips that included an 8K read-only memory (ROM), a 256-word random access memory chip, and a 1K programmable read-only memory (PROM).

Bowler summed up the benefits of TBI in the Conclusion section of his S.A.E. paper this way:

"The beneficial features of General Motor's [sic] TBI have made this new system an active contender for future engine control applications. These features include hardware simplicity, reduced evaporative emissions, excellent hot fuel handling characteristics, a single metering circuit to calibrate per throttle bore, elimination of ignition off dieseling (run on), full fuel range scheduling including cold start, altitude compensation (with EGR compensation), and the flexibility to expand to closed loop with an exhaust sensor."

The GM Throttle Body Fuel Injection System was introduced on the 1980 Cadillac Eldorado and Seville, in keeping with corporate precedent to introduce the latest technological developments on its premiere car line. The other GM divisions quickly followed, and TBI applications spread to trucks as well as cars during the eighties.

"Everybody figured throttle body injection wouldn't fly because it was nothing but a force-fed carburetor," said Bill Howell. "When you run it on the dynamometer it doesn't look like anything. When you measure the various parameters such as mixture distribution and brake-specific fuel consumption, it doesn't look like anything. But, when you put it against the best emission-controlled carburetor we had in 1979, '80

Cross-Fire Injection was Chevrolet's high performance application of Throttle Body Injection. The 305 ci Z/28 and 350 ci Corvette were the first Chevrolets to receive TBI in 1982. Two staggered throttle body injectors sat atop a plenum-type manifold. This induction system was reminiscent of the optional 2 x 4 bbl system available on the 1967-1969 Z/28. Chevrolet

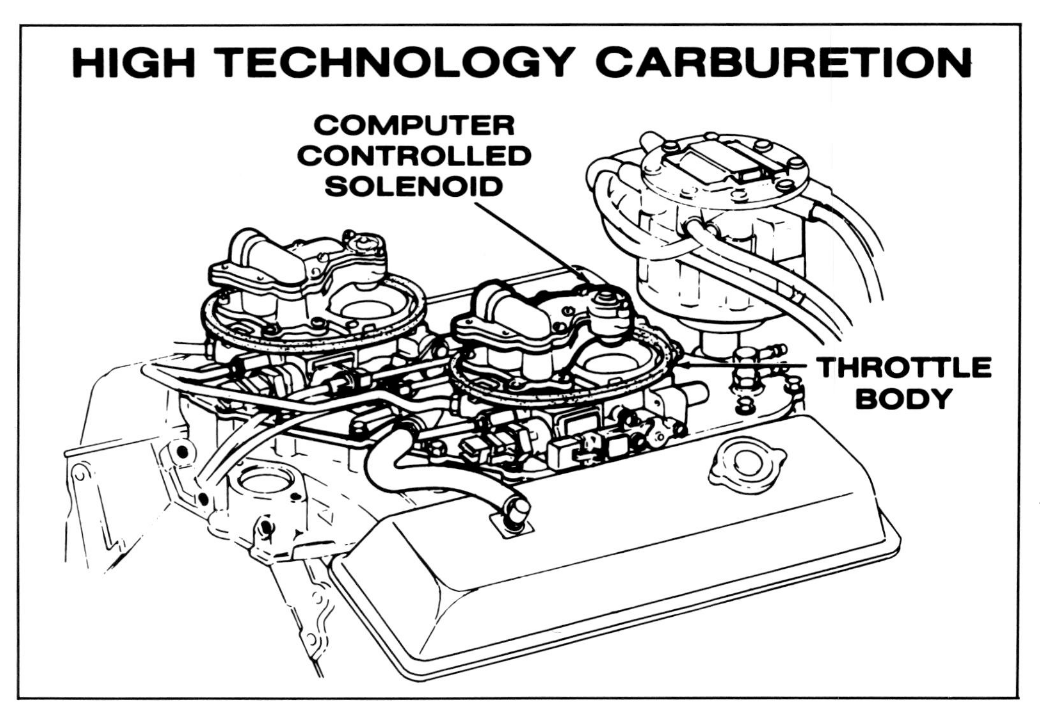

TBI offered much more precise fuel metering for the small-block, improving emissions, drivability and performance. Cross-Fire Injection was optional on the 305 ci V-8 in the Z/28 for 1982 and 1983, and standard on the 350 ci V-8 in the 1982 and 1984 Corvette. The Corvette wasn't built in 1983 while the factory changed over to produce the all-new 1984 model. Chevrolet

and '81, the car drove worlds better with throttle body fuel injection. It translates to something that's measurable in car fuel economy and driveability and the customers love it."

TBI was first offered on the small-block V-8 in 1982 Camaros and Corvettes. Chevrolet developed a high-performance application of TBI which it called Cross-Fire Injection. It featured two TBI units mounted in a staggered position on a new plenum-type intake manifold. In appearance and concept, it harkened back to the days in the late sixties when the 2 × 4 bbl induction system was offered in the Z-28, but it by no means developed that kind of power.

"We got the job of having two of them," Louis Cuttitta said of the throttle body injectors. "We couldn't have one; we had to have dual TBI for the Corvette [and Z-28]. When we got it, we were told we couldn't change it. Instead, we sent a bunch of guys off to school to learn how this thing works so we could calibrate it—meaning computer chips. We got it to the point where we could get the car to run and meet fuel economy and emissions requirements. But, lo and behold, when we took the car on a trip during cold weather, you would go about fifty feet and it would stall. What we finally found out was the throttle bodies were icing. Ice would form on the throttle bodies to the point it would restrict air flow. You had to open the throttle to the point of being ridiculous and it would stall. This throttle body icing almost killed the conception because these two throttle bodies were located essentially out over the valve covers and there was no way to get any exhaust heat up there as you could with a carburetor."

The reason for this was the intake manifold Cuttitta and his team of technicians were forced to use—an intake manifold with a very interesting history. Because of cost restraints, a new manifold could not be designed but an existing design had to be adapted for use with the two throttle body injectors.

"Remember the original Z-28 Camaro that Penske raced? It had two Holley four-barrels on it. Not the 2 × 4 manifold that was the one on the [production] line. The one where the carburetors sat out over the valve covers. *That* inlet manifold was what we got stuck with for the TBI! The throttle bodies were just adapted to that manifold, because they already had the dies and the money spent.

"We developed it so there was more hot air to the air cleaner, called 'Thermac,' and that sort of saved it. We never liked TBI because the throttle bodies were the wrong way. The throttle shafts were parallel to the crankshaft, and they should have been the other way. If they had been the other way, we would have gained distribution and many other things, but it was too late to change."

There was another problem with Cross Fire Injection that surfaced during pilot testing of the Z-28 prior to production. It was known among Chevrolet engineers as the infamous "Robo Car Wash

Tuned-Port Injection replaced Cross-Fire Injection on the 1985 Corvette. The RPO engine code was L-98. In its first year of production, this 350 ci V-8 was rated at 230 hp at 4000 rpm with 330 lb-ft of torque at 3200 rpm. TPI qualified the small-block as perhaps the most handsome V-8 to come from Chevrolet. Chevrolet

This exploded assembly of the 350 ci small-block clearly shows the Cross-Fire Injection system as installed in the 1984 Corvette. Many hours of flow-testing went into the design of the plenum manifold for optimum mixture distribution, torque and horsepower. The Cross-Fire Injection air cleaner and cover were unique to the 1984. The engine was rated at 205 hp with a 9.0:1 compression ratio. Chevrolet

The Monte Carlo made its debut in 1970 as Chevrolet's full-size luxury coupe and by the mid-1980s it was also Chevrolet's winning NASCAR Winston Cup racer. Darrell Waltrip swept the series in 1985 and Dale Earnhardt took the 1986 crown, both at the wheels of Monte Carlo-based stockers. Chevrolet responded with an SS package for the Monte Carlo complete with a stealth black paint scheme and brilliant red racing stripes.

incident." When this car, with its fresh air hood, was sent through a Robo Car Wash, the high-pressure water jets forced open the flaps in the fresh air hood and water poured into the Cross Fire Injection air cleaner—literally flooding the engine. Chevrolet engineers tried various quick fixes, but there was not enough time to redesign the hood intake to solve the problem.

Cross-Fire Injection was optional in the Z-28 and standard in the Corvette that year. In the Z-28, Cross-Fire Injection came on the 305-ci small-block (the 350-ci V-8 was not available) and was rated at 165 hp at 4200 rpm with 240 lb-ft of torque at 2400 rpm. By comparison, the standard 305-ci V-8 in the Z-28 with 8.6:1 cr was rated at 145 hp at 4000 rpm with 240 lb-ft of torque at 2000 rpm. The Cross-Fire Injection option in the Z-28 was $450. In the Corvette, this essentially new 350-ci V-8 received the RPO engine code L83. With 200 hp at 4200 rpm and 285 lb-ft of torque at 2800 rpm, it had ten more horsepower than the four-barrel 350-ci L81 V-8 of 1981.

Chevrolet engineers were not entirely comfortable with the name Cross-Fire Injection. Borrowing from the Turbo-Fire label of the sixties, Cross-Fire Injection was selected after many proposals and the requisite market testing to describe how each TBI unit on the plenum manifold fed the cylinder bank on the opposite side of the engine. When *Road & Track* editor Joe Rusz was asked by Chevrolet engineers what the name signified to him during a new-model introduction at the Milford Proving Grounds, his response was "Ignition interference caused by induction." The magazine did a full road test on the 1982 Corvette with the L83 and couldn't help having a little fun with the name. "One test driver commented that this sounds more like an engine malfunction than a sales feature (Stand back, kid, that engine's about to cross-fire!) but the system works very well nevertheless," the editors wrote.

Despite the new induction system, performance was still down from the sixties heydays. The 1982 Corvette reached 60 mph in 7.9 seconds and covered the quarter-mile in 16.1 seconds doing 84.5 mph.

While TBI appeared to be the wave of the future, the four-barrel carburetor was by no means gone. In fact, performance development work was begun on a High Output 305 V-8 to boost the small-block's power in the Z-28 and appeal to those enthusiasts who wanted performance with a four-barrel carburetor.

The L69

Chevrolet engineers decided to develop a truly high-output small-block V-8 with four-barrel carburetor based on the

305. Rochester was put to work to develop a carburetor to suit this package. A compression ratio of 9.5:1 was selected, and camshafts were tested until one was selected on the basis of its ability to deliver power as well as emissions. Additional steps were made in the intake system with the use of a dual-snorkel air cleaner, and in the exhaust system to get additional horsepower by the use of larger diameter exhaust and tailpipes behind a wide-mouth, lower-restriction catalytic converter used in the Corvette.

The High Output 305 V-8 was to be available in the Z-28 and the Monte Carlo. In the Monte Carlo, the engine had a compression ratio of 8.6:1 and was rated at 180 hp at 4800 rpm with 235 lb-ft of torque at 3200 rpm. For the engine used in the Z-28, the rating was 190 hp at 4800 rpm with 240 lb-ft of torque at 3200 rpm. This engine, like all of Chevrolet's engines, had to have an RPO number, but it turned out to be no easy process.

"When we went to what would ultimately be the Camaro high-performance package," Denny Davis said, "I was told to go back and get one of the old high-performance RPO numbers that were no longer used and put it on this 305 four-barrel package. Well, GM, in its infinite wisdom, reused those old RPO numbers for something else after they went out of production. So all the old high-performance numbers that we had back in the sixties had been assigned to other packages.

"So I said, 'OK, guys, if you can't give me any of those, give me a new RPO number to go with this engine.' So they came up with some lousy number, and I called them up and said, 'Guys, this stinks. This has got no pizazz at all. After all the other Z packages and everything we've had, I want something with sex appeal. Get me something with sex appeal. Get me something other than this thing.' Engine RPOs were now into Ls. We had L engine designations whether we wanted them or not. So they called my boss . . . and came back to me with the L69. I never told my boss what the RPO number was until it was in print. At GM, once something's rolling, it's like an elephant—it's hard to stop. I knew if I didn't tell anybody it would get far enough, because I got a big kick out of it. They thought I would holler; I just laughed. I thought, "That's beautiful. I love it, guys. I'm going to leave it.' So I just kept sending it through until it got entrenched enough to the point that if anybody conservative might have figured out what it was, it was too late."

The L69 replaced the Cross-Fire Injection 305 in the 1984 Z-28 as the top optional engine, but it was an expensive option: $530. After a one-year hiatus, the Corvette returned, new from the ground up for 1984. This was the last year the Cross-Fire Injection 350-ci V-8 was offered in America's only sports car. Some-

In 1988 Chevrolet replaced the four-barrel carburetor on 305 ci V-8s offered in Camaros with a single throttle body injector. The TBI was mounted on a conventional cast iron intake manifold. Engine RPO code was LO3. Rating was 170 hp at 4000 rpm with 255 lb-ft of torque at 2400 rpm. The High Output 305 ci four-barrel V-8 (RPO engine code L69) was last offered in 1986. Chevrolet

Tuned-Port Injection was initially developed for the 5.0 liter (305 ci) V-8 but was adapted to the 5.7 liter (350 ci) V-8 when Chevrolet decided not to drop the larger displacement small-block. This cutaway illustration shows the path intake air takes through the throttle plates, into the plenum, along the tuned runners and intake manifold and finally the cylinder head intake ports where the fuel is injected. Shown is the 350 ci L-98. Chevrolet

CORVETTE
BOSCH
GOODYEAR

RACING
SCCA PRO RACING
CHALLENGE
L A SPEED
MID AMERICA
BOSCH
GOODYEAR
ZF
BILSTEIN
SHOCK ABSORBERS

Previous page
Corvette Challenge action from 1989 with a small-block-powered Corvette up on two wheels. This series provided for some of the most technically advanced performance tuning the Chevrolet small-block V-8 ever received. Jack Hiles

thing better was coming. Something called Tuned Port Injection.

Tuned Port Injection

In 1982, Denny Davis was promoted from his position as supervisor of the basic engine group to the newly-formed advanced engine design group. A radically new induction system for the small-block V-8 started to take shape in the basic engine group under the direction of Frank Langenstein. It all came about with a push to make the 305-ci V-8 the largest displacement V-8 available in the Camaro and Corvette in the future. Davis recalled the story.

"Because of constraints on fuel economy, we would get edicts: 'You are not going to have engines larger than 305 cubic inches.' That's really how the 305 high-performance stuff got developed. It was going to be *the* engine size—including the Corvette. The fuel injection package was developed for the 305. I tried to develop the fuel injection package for a 350 and I was told, 'Keep this up and you're going to be fired. It's going to be sized for the 305 cubic inch engine. That's the biggest engine it's ever going on, you're not going to get the 350 cubic inch engine, so don't worry about it.' And I said, 'I don't believe you guys, because this happens at the eleventh hour all the time.'

"So we developed the 305 along those auspices and, of course, guess what happened? Along came the Corvette. They said, 'We want that performance. We don't want to lose our image. We want the most potent machine we can get. We can handle 350 cubic inches. Put it on the 350.' So it was sized for the 305 and incorporated on the 350 after the fact. That was the reason the 305 got any high-performance development at all. I was

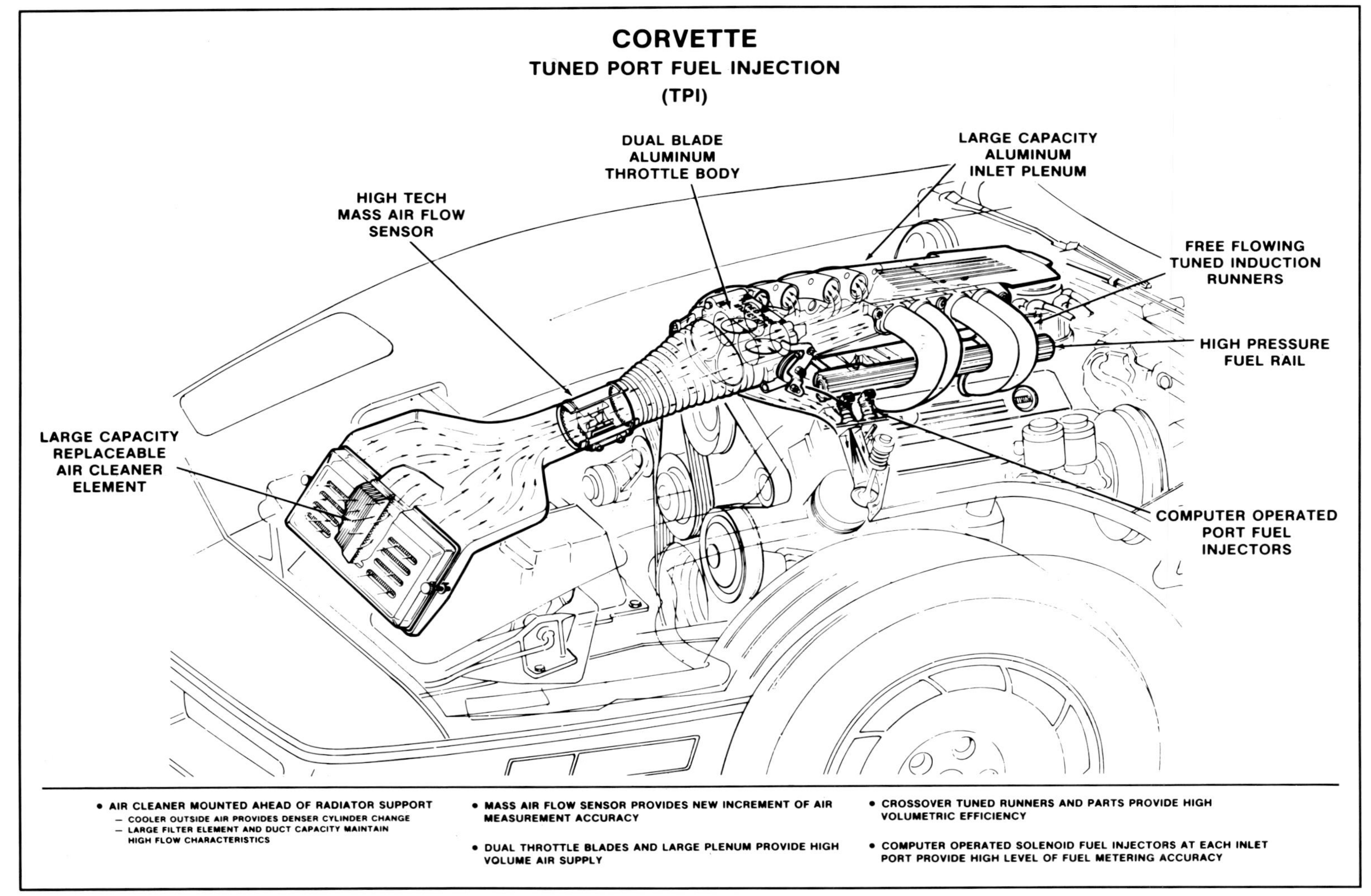

This illustration shows the key components of Tuned-Port Injection as installed on the Corvette. TPI harnessed the technology of the eighties with proven tuned induction runner concepts. The fresh air intake is a lasting legacy of Vince Piggins now used industry-wide. Chevrolet

In 1990 model year Corvettes such as this convertible, the L98 engine with Tuned-Port Injection produced 245 hp at 4000 rpm when the engine was teamed with the 6-speed manual transmission. An extra 5 hp was available to buyers of coupes with 3.07:1 axle ratios since those coupes were fitted with slightly less restrictive mufflers that were considered too loud for convertibles. Stealing the Corvette thunder in 1990, however, was the ZR-1 model with its LT5 engine, which was definitely not a small-block. Chevrolet

the first four months. It really surprised a lot of people."

Chevrolet engineers at The Raceshop were in for an even bigger surprise when Covey received a letter one day from a professional racer who had installed the engine in one of his race cars to compete in the 24 Hours of Daytona—with impressive results.

"We weren't trying to create a race engine," Covey said honestly, "although we did have somebody run one at the 24 Hours of Daytona in 1990 and finished seventh in the race, which I think is pretty amazing. This guy ran in the GTO class. He had run race engines every year prior and had blown every race engine he had taken down there. So they figured, 'We're just going to bolt this sucker in—what have we got to lose? If it blows up, we've lost three grand. If we blew up a race motor, we'd lose thirty grand.' He said they were down a little bit in the straightaway speeds compared to a full-blown race engine, but he said he went the twenty-four hours and that's the first time they had ever done that. I think that says a lot about the engine."

It may be hard for some to fathom that a street engine could not only compete in but survive the 24 Hours of Daytona, but it happened, nevertheless. Chevrolet has every intention of refining it and making it better still, while keeping the engine affordable.

"This engine, like any Chevrolet engine, is going to go through some evolution," Covey said of the 5.7 liter H.O.'s future. With product offerings like this, the Chevrolet small-block enthusiast has an exciting future to look forward to.

A Dynamic Decade

In terms of performance, the 1980s marked a return to performance that had been absent for much of the seventies. In addition, the small-block proved it was up to every demand made of it in the area of emissions and fuel economy. In short, the small-block V-8 could be anything Chevrolet wanted it to be. However, had not computer technology come along to save it, the small-block story, certainly in terms of performance, might have been different.

As a toast to the return of performance and a send-off of the eighties, *Car & Driver* tested a 1989 Corvette convertible with the 245-hp L98 for the June 1989 issue. The car was fitted with the rakish factory removable hardtop. This Corvette was as far a cry from the ragtop Corvette of the sixties with its fuel-injected 327-ci V-8 as one could imagine, the only thing in common being the small-block itself. But then, the prices were somewhat different, too, with the 1989 version going for over $40,000 as tested.

The editors wrote glowingly of the Corvette, "We're more than happy to live with an occasional computer-controlled upshift in order to enjoy the fruits of the new ZF box. Suddenly, a manual-transmission Corvette is worth having again.

tional Race of Champions, and thus wear the IROC badge. Chevrolet went back to using Z28 for its high-performance Camaro.

The Caprice was completely redesigned, with an aerodynamic envelope that cut its drag coefficient from 0.41 to 0.33. The TBI 170-hp 305-ci V-8 (RPO LO3) managed to achieve an EPA estimated city mileage of 17 mpg with an impressive 26 mpg estimated highway mileage. Only the police could get the 350 small-block in their Caprices. MVMA Specifications listed this as Police Vehicle SEO 9C1. The engine was the LO5 with TBI having a 9.8:1 compression ratio, developing 195 hp at 4400 rpm with 290 lb-ft of torque at 2400 rpm, running through a single exhaust. The axle ratio was 3.41, compared to the Caprice's standard 2.56 and optional 3.08.

The broad range of powertrains for the Camaro continued for 1991. Standard in the RS convertible was the 170-hp 305-ci V-8 (RPO LO3) having the 5-sp manual transmission with a 3.08 axle ratio. Optional was the same engine with 4-sp automatic transmission with a 2.73 axle ratio. In the RS coupe, the standard engine was the 3.1 liter V-6 (RPO LHO) with the 5-sp manual transmission and 3.42 axle ratio. Optional powertrains in the coupe included the 3.1 liter V-6 with the 4-sp automatic transmission and 3.23 axle ratio, the 170-hp 305 with 5-sp manual transmission and 3.08 axle ratio, and the same engine with the 4-sp automatic transmission with a 2.73 axle ratio.

In the Z28 coupe and convertible, the standard powertrain was the 205-hp TPI 305 V-8 with 5-sp manual transmission with 3.08 axle ratio. Optional in the convertible was the same engine with the 4-sp automatic transmission with 2.73 axle ratio. There were three optional powertrains in the Z28 coupe. These included the 205-hp TPI 305 V-8 with 4-sp automatic transmission and 2.73 axle ratio; the 230-hp TPI 305 V-8 with 5-sp manual transmission and 3.42 axle ratio; and the 245-hp TPI 350 V-8 (RPO B2L) with 4-sp automatic transmission and 3.23 axle ratiio. The manual transmission was not available on the TPI 350 V-8 in the Z28.

There were four small-block V-8 powertrain combinations available in the Corvette for 1991. Standard in the Corvette coupe and convertible was the 245-hp L98 TPI 350 V-8 with 4-sp automatic transmission and 2.59 axle ratio. Optional

The detail differences between the TPI V-8 for the Z/28 and Corvette are visible in these two photos. The B2L for the Z/28 gets cast iron cylinder heads, cast iron exhaust manifolds, stamped valve covers and different serpentine belt and pulley system. Output for 1991 was 245 hp at 4400 rpm with 345 lb-ft of torque at 3200 rpm. MVMA total dressed engine dry weight for 1991 was 627 pounds. Chevrolet

The L98 for Corvettes featured cast aluminum cylinder heads, steel tube exhaust manifolds, different valve covers and serpentine belt and pulley system unique to the Corvette. Output for 1991 was 250 hp at 4400 rpm with 350 lb-ft of torque at 3200 rpm. MVMA total dressed engine dry weight for 1991 was 557 lbs. Engine shown is bolted to a ZF (Zahnradfabrik Friedrichshafen) six-speed manual transmission built in Germany, available only in the Corvette. Chevrolet

Despite having the same 350 ci displacement, 4.40 bore spacing, 9.03 in. cylinder block deck height and 19.93 in. cylinder block length, the LT5 for the ZR-1 Corvette is not a member of the small-block family. Bore is 3.90 in. and stroke 3.66 in. The cylinder block, cylinder heads, entire induction system and even oil pan are cast aluminum. With an 11.0:1 compression ratio, the 32-valve LT5 was rated at 375 hp at 5800 rpm with 370 lb-ft of torque at 4800 rpm for 1991. MVMA total dressed engine dry weight is 596 lbs. Chevrolet

in the coupe and convertible was the 250-hp L98 TPI 350 V-8 with 6-sp manual transmission and 3.45 axle ratio. The other optional powertrain in the coupe was the 250-hp L98 with 4-sp automatic transmission and 3.07 axle ratio. The other optional powertrain in the convertible was the 245-hp L98 with 4-sp automatic transmission and 2.73 axle ratio. Of course, for those for whom money was no object, one could order the 345-hp LT5 as installed in the ZR1 Corvette, but again, this engine is not of the small-block family.

The LT1 for 1992

In the late eighties, the engineers at Chevrolet and GM Powertrain began work on significant changes to the small-block to further improve performance, fuel economy, emissions and durability. These changes would permit the engine to be available well into the next century. The changes and improvements envisioned were so comprehensive, the project was given the name GEN II. Nevertheless, a small-block it would remain. Chevrolet realized that discarding the proven small-block platform for something new would be a mistake. There is no more loyal a group of enthusiasts than small-block fans.

Attention was focused on improving the performance of the base 350-ci V-8 in the Corvette, the L98. As mentioned earlier, Tuned Port Injection was origi-

The base V-8 in Camaros and Caprices in the late 1980s and early 1990s is the 305 ci V-8 (RPO LO3) with a dual-throat model 220 throttle body injector on a cast aluminum intake manifold. Output varies with the model and transmission. The 305 V-8 fitted with Tuned-Port Injection has the engine code RPO LB9. MVMA total dressed engine dry weight is 606.5 lbs with automatic transmission and 641 lbs with manual transmission. Chevrolet

The small-block V-8 has been a staple in Chevrolet trucks for decades. Carburetors are gone from small-blocks installed in trucks, replaced with electronic fuel injection. The 350 ci V-8 gets the job done in this 1991 extended cab 4 x 4 Sportside pickup. Chevrolet

nally developed for the 305-ci V-8 and adapted to the 350-ci V-8. While the TPI 350 small-block was a vast improvement over the Cross Fire Injection 350, it was not ideal. The engineers at Chevrolet felt the TPI L98 could be improved upon. Anil Kulkarni of GM Powertrain was Chief Engineer for the project. Research and development was focused on these key areas: induction (including cylinder heads), coolant flow, ignition and exhaust. As with any project of this nature, it was a closely guarded secret and details of this engine were not released until the long-lead Corvette press review in the summer of 1991 in Montreal, Canada.

When the hoods were raised on the 1992 Corvettes, the automotive press saw an engine radically different in appearance from the L98 that had powered the car since 1985. Gone were the induction plenum, tubes and manifold that had become familiar during the previous seven years. They were replaced by a low-rise, one-piece cast aluminum intake manifold. This new intake manifold eliminated the water crossover between the cylinder heads, effectively lowering the overall height of the engine by 3.50 in. Coupled to the intake manifold was a new throttle body and low-restriction air snorkle. The high pressure fuel rail on each side of the manifold fed gas to the AC Rochester Multec fuel injectors; these injectors showed an improvement over previous units by giving more precise fuel flow and a spray pattern matched to this specific engine's power output. Two black covers bearing the car's name spanned the area between the valve covers and induction manifold.

The editors and writers noticed another feature of this new engine—the High Energy Ignition (HEI) housing at the rear of the engine was gone. In its place was a new optical sensor-type ignition at the front of the engine. A new precision-cast and machined aluminum front cover housed the new gear-driven water pump and optical distributor. The distributor housing featured a stainless steel shutter wheel that was driven by a shaft off the camshaft sprocket. Light shining through this shutter wheel produced 360 pulses per crankshaft revolution. These signals were fed to the Powertrain Control Module that precisely issued the spark timing commands. The net result of this effort was the most precise ignition timing, which reduced emissions, improved power and optimized fuel economy.

A major feature of this new engine—dubbed the LT1 after its legendary namesake—was its reverse-flow cooling system. The system was designed to route coolant first through the cylinder heads after making a brief passage through the engine block to better cool the cylinder head and intake manifold. It then passes to the engine block and around the cylinder bores, and finally back to the water pump before it repeats the procedure or is directed to the radiator. The gear-driven water pump was designed to eliminate the constant side load on the bearings and seals of standard water pumps that eventually results in leaks.

CHEVROLET

Previous page
The year 1991 marked the return of the Z/28 when the Chevrolet had to relinquish the IROC identification to another manufacturer. The Z/28 (foreground) is distinguished from the Camaro RS by its higher rear spoiler. The Tuned-Port Injection 305 ci V-8 was practically as fast as the TPI 350 ci V-8. Chevrolet

The LO3 (305 ci) V-8 as installed in the 1991 Caprice. With a 9.3:1 compression ratio, output that year was 170 hp at 4200 rpm with 255 lb-ft of torque at 2400 rpm. Air cleaner differed from that on the LO3 installed in Camaros. Engine is shown bolted to the 700-R4 Hydramatic four-speed overdrive automatic transmission. Chevrolet

This reverse-flow concept necessitated redesigning the engine block and cylinder heads extensively, so these major components are unique to the LT1 and are not interchangeable with earlier small-block pieces. Reverse-flow cooling produces higher cylinder bore temperatures and reduced ring bore friction, reducing wear and increasing mileage.

The cylinder heads received extensive research and development in the intake and exhaust port to improve flow. This was carefully matched to the design of the intake manifold and exhaust manifolds. Intake and exhaust valve diameter was unchanged from the L98—1.94 and

The 350 ci V-8 has been a small-block staple in Chevrolet trucks for decades. In 1987, throttle body injection (TBI) replaced carburetion. Note the different exhaust manifolds from those on passenger car 350 V-8s. This engine is from 1991. Chevrolet

See the U.S.A. in Your Chevrolet! The small-block V-8 engineering legacy of Ed Cole, Harry Barr and Al Kolbe launched in 1955 continues into the 1990s. This 1991 Caprice Classic LTZ is powered by the 305 ci V-8 with TBI. The 350 ci V-8 is offered in the Police Package available only to state and local law enforcement agencies. Chevrolet

1.50 in, respectively. For this engine, Chevrolet returned to cast iron exhaust manifolds, doing away with the steel tube headers fitted to the L98.

Performance of the LT1 was improved even further with revised camshaft specifications. Intake and exhaust valve lift were both 0.450 in, compared to the L98's 0.415 for the intake and 0.430 for the exhaust.

The exhaust system was designed to improve flow and reduce emissions even further. This was achieved, according to the Corvette press literature, using "new dual oxygen sensors, two high-efficiency catalysts and an electric air injection pump . . . Placing a catalytic converter and an oxygen sensor on each engine bank allows greater control of the fuel-air mixture and spark timing for improved engine performance. The new catalysts are close-coupled and located in the engine compartment, which improves light-off and conversion efficiency. And low-restriction, three-way converters reduce back pressure, thus providing for high engine power."

All these refinements and improvements made the LT1 the most powerful production small-block V-8 that Chevrolet had ever offered in a passenger car. Performance increases over the L98 were substantial. The LT1 was rated at 300 net hp at 5000 rpm with 330 lb-ft of torque at 4000 rpm. This was achieved while increasing mileage by one mile per gallon at the same time! With the four-speed automatic transmission the Corvette reached 60 mph in 5.26 seconds and covered the quarter mile in 13.9 seconds at 102.2 mph. With the six-speed manual transmission, the Corvette reached 60 mph in a breathtaking 4.92 seconds and covered the quarter mile in 13.7 seconds at 103.5 mph. These are arguably the fastest times posted by a factory small-block Corvette in the car's history.

The LT1 is indicative of where the small-block V-8 is going in the future. It is reassuring to a new generation of small-block enthusiasts that the performance capabilities of this engine will be maintained and improved regardless of government regulations. Advanced technology allows the small-block to meet these challenges while giving buyers what they want. The Chevrolet small-block V-8—born in the mid-twentieth century—will meet the demands of the twenty-first century with aplomb.

GM Powertrain and Chevrolet worked closely together in the development of the 350 ci V-8 LT1. The engine incorporates the latest electronic engine controls, redesigned intake manifold with tuned-port injection, reverse-flow cooling, close-coupled catalytic converters and other refinements to make it the most powerful small-block that Chevrolet has ever built. Chevrolet

This cutaway shows the radically new components of the 300 hp 350 ci LT1 V-8. The extensive research and development program to boost the small-block's power while reducing emissions and maintenance needs proves that Chevrolet is committed to seeing the small-block V-8 will be around for decades to come. Chevrolet

The Chevrolet small-block V-8 as developed by The Raceshop develops 650 hp for use in NASCAR events. The small-block is easily modified to comply with rules of various race-sanctioning groups. The Chevrolet Raceshop has an ongoing research and development program to release small-block parts for racers. Chevrolet

Next page
The 300 hp LT1 350 ci V-8 made the 1992 Corvette the fastest small-block V-8-powered Chevy to come off the assembly line. The LT1 made the Corvette a match for some of the world's fastest and most expensive sports cars. The technology that makes the LT1 so powerful will see to it that Chevrolet's flagship will meet the 21st century with aplomb. Chevrolet

Appendix

Small-block Basic Specifications and Production Years

Disp.	Bore	Stroke	B/S Ratio	Production Years
262 ci	3.67 in.	3.10 in.	1.18	1975
265 ci	3.75 in.	3.00 in.	1.25	1955-1956
267 ci	3.50 in.	3.48 in.	1.03	1979-1982
283 ci	3.87 in.	3.00 in.	1.29	1957-1967
302 ci	4.00 in.	3.00 in.	1.33	1967-1969
305 ci	3.75 in.	3.48 in.	1.08	1976-Present
307 ci	3.87 in.	3.25 in.	1.19	1968-1973
327 ci	4.00 in.	3.25 in.	1.23	1962-1969
350 ci	4.00 in.	3.48 in.	1.15	1967-Present
400 ci	4.12 in.	3.75 in.	1.10	1970-1976

Note: Production years are for passenger cars only. Some of these engines continued to be used in trucks, vans or industrial applications after passenger car production stopped.

Small-block Crankshaft Specifications

Disp.	Main Journal Dia.	Rod Journal Dia.	Main Bearing Cap
262 ci	2.45 in.	2.10 in.	2-bolt
265 ci	2.30 in.	2.00 in.	2-bolt
267 ci	2.45 in.	2.10 in.	2-bolt
283 ci	2.30 in.	2.00 in.	2-bolt
302 ci (1967)	2.30 in.	2.00 in.	2-bolt
302 ci (1968-1969)	2.45 in.	2.10 in.	4-bolt
305 ci	2.45 in.	2.10 in.	2-bolt
307 ci	2.45 in.	2.10 in.	2-bolt
327 ci (1962-1967)	2.30 in.	2.00 in.	2-bolt
327 ci (1968-1969)	2.45 in.	2.10 in.	2-bolt
350 ci	2.45 in.	2.10 in.	2-bolt & 4-bolt
400 ci (1970-1972)	2.65 in.	2.10 in.	4-bolt
400 ci (1973-1976)	2.65 in.	2.10 in.	2-bolt

Small-block V-8 Technical Specifications

Engine:	TBI 305 V-8 (RPO LO3)	TPI 305 V-8 (RPO LB9)	TPI 350 V-8 (RPO L98)
Bore	3.74 in.	3.74 in.	4.00 in.
Stroke	3.48 in.	3.48 in.	3.48 in.
Bore spacing	4.40 in.	4.40 in.	4.40 in.
Cyl. Blk. Deck Ht.	9.025 in.	9.025 in.	9.025 in.
Cyl. Blk. Length	20.19 in.	20.19 in.	19.93 in.
Cyl. Blk. Material	Cast Iron	Cast Iron	Cast Iron
Cyl. Blk. Weight	151.4 lbs.	151.4 lbs.	151.5 lbs.
Cyl. Head Material	Cast Iron	Cast Iron	Cast Iron (Camaro) Aluminum (Corvette)
Cyl. Head Weight	43.7 lbs.	43.7 lbs.	43.7 lbs. (Iron) 22.0 lbs. (Alum.)
Combustion Chamber Volume	55.2 cc	55.2 cc	55.9 cc
Int. Valve Diameter	1.84 in.	1.84 in.	1.94 in.
Exh. Valve Diameter	1.50 in.	1.50 in.	1.50 in.
Crankshaft	Nodular Cast Iron	Nodular Cast Iron	Nodular Cast Iron
Crankshaft Weight	51.5 lbs.	51.5 lbs.	51.5 lbs.
Piston	Cast Aluminum	Cast Aluminum	Forged Aluminum
Connecting Rod	Steel	Steel	Steel
Con. Rod Centers	5.7 in.	5.7 in.	5.7 in.
Intake Manifold	Cast Aluminum	Cast Aluminum	Cast Aluminun
Intake Manifold Weight	15.2 lbs.	13.5 lbs.	13.5 lbs.
Exhaust Manifold	Cast Iron	Cast Iron	Cast Iron (Camaro) Steel (Corvette)
Exhaust Manifold Weight	9.6 lbs. (LH) 8.4 lbs. (RH)	9.8 lbs. (LH) 8.4 lbs. (RH)	8.0 lbs. ea. (Corvette)
Fuel System	Throttle Body Injection	Inlet Port Fuel Injection	Inlet Port Fuel Injection
System Pressure	11.0 psi	44 psi	43.5 psi
Total Engine Weight	606.5 lbs. (w. Auto. Trans.) 641.1 lbs. (w. Manual Trans.)	623 lbs. (w. Auto Trans.) 657 lbs. (w. Manual Trans.)	627 lbs. (w. Auto. Trans.)

Source: Motor Vehicle Manufacturers Association for 1991 models
Note: The L98 was installed in the Corvette having aluminum cylinder heads. The comparable engine available in the Camaro came with cast iron cylinder heads with the engine code RPO B2L.

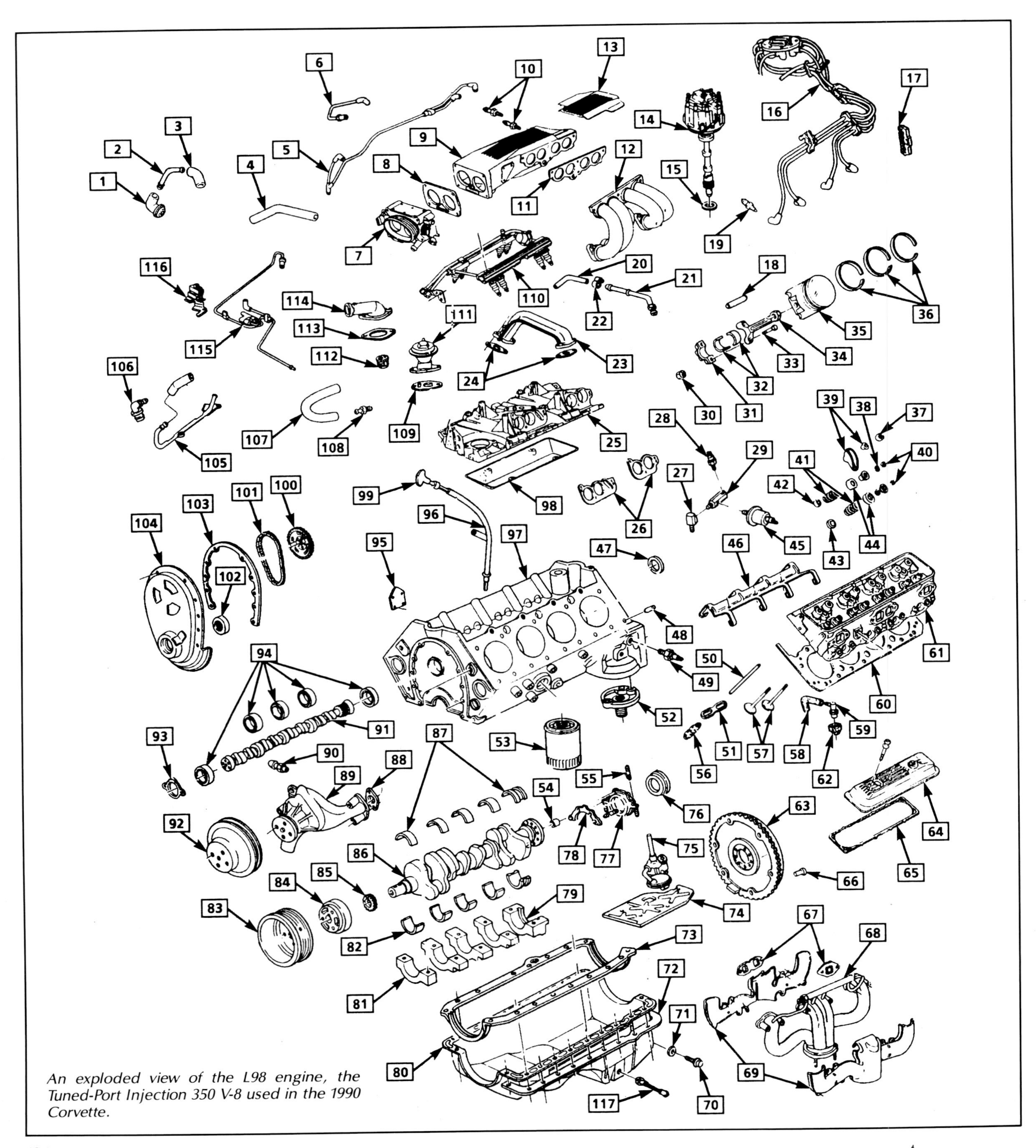

An exploded view of the L98 engine, the Tuned-Port Injection 350 V-8 used in the 1990 Corvette.

1	CRANKCASE VENTILATION TUBE GROMMET
2	CRANKCASE VENTILATION TUBE
3	CRANKCASE VENTILATION TUBE CONNECTOR
4	HEATER INLET HOSE
5	AIR INJECTION CONTROL VALVE VACUUM HARNESS
6	EXHAUST EMISSION CONTROL VACUUM - REAR HARNESS
7	THROTTLE BODY
8	THROTTLE BODY GASKET
9	INTAKE MANIFOLD PLENUM
10	INTAKE MANIFOLD VACUUM FITTING
11	INTAKE MANIFOLD PLENUM GASKET
12	INTAKE MANIFOLD TUBE
13	INTAKE MANIFOLD PLENUM EXTENSION
14	IGNITION DISTRIBUTOR
15	DISTRIBUTOR GASKET
16	SPARK PLUG WIRE HARNESS
17	SPARK PLUG WIRE RETAINER
18	PISTON PIN
19	SPARK PLUG
20	MANIFOLD VAPOR HOSE
21	MANIFOLD VAPOR TUBING
22	MANIFOLD VAPOR HOSE CLAMP
23	EGR VALVE PIPE
24	EGR VALVE PIPE GASKET
25	INTAKE MANIFOLD
26	INTAKE MANIFOLD TUBE GASKET
27	OIL PRESSURE GAGE SENSOR FITTING
28	OIL PRESSURE SWITCH
29	ENGINE OIL PRESSURE GAGE SENSOR FITTING
30	CONNECTING ROD NUT
31	CONNECTING ROD CAP
32	CONNECTING ROD BEARING INSERT
33	CONNECTING ROD BOLT
34	CONNECTING ROD
35	ENGINE PISTON
36	PISTON RING
37	VALVE ROCKER ARM ADJUST NUT
38	VALVE STEM OIL SEAL
39	VALVE ROCKER ARM AND BALL
40	VALVE STEM KEY
41	VALVE (W/DAMPER) SPRING
42	INLET VALVE STEM (W/RETAINER) SEAL
43	VALVE SPRING SHIM
44	VALVE STEM OIL SHIELD
45	OIL PRESSURE SENSOR
46	VALVE LIFTER RESTRICTOR RETAINER
47	EXPANSION PLUG
48	DOWEL PIN
49	OIL TEMPERATURE SENSOR
50	VALVE PUSHROD
51	VALVE LIFTER GUIDE
52	OIL FILTER BY-PASS VALVE ADAPTER
53	OIL FILTER
54	CLUTCH PILOT BEARING
55	STUD
56	HYDRAULIC VALVE LIFTER
57	VALVES
58	CRANKCASE VENTILATION VALVE HOSE
59	CRANKCASE VENTILATION VALVE
60	CYLINDER HEAD GASKET
61	CYLINDER HEAD
62	CRANKCASE VENTILATION GROMMET
63	CRANKSHAFT FLYWHEEL
64	VALVE ROCKER COVER
65	VALVE ROCKER COVER GASKET
66	GROOVE PIN

67	EXHAUST MANIFOLD GASKET
68	EXHAUST MANIFOLD
69	EXHAUST MANIFOLD HEATER SHIELD
70	OIL PAN DRAIN PLUG
71	DRAIN PLUG GASKET
72	OIL PAN REINFORCEMENT
73	OIL PAN GASKET
74	OIL PAN BAFFLE
75	OIL PUMP
76	CRANKSHAFT - REAR SEAL
77	CRANKSHAFT REAR SEAL RETAINER
78	CRANKSHAFT REAR SEAL RETAINER GASKET
79	CRANKSHAFT REAR BEARING CAP
80	OIL PAN
81	CRANKSHAFT BEARING CAP
82	CRANKSHAFT LOWER BEARINGS
83	CRANKSHAFT PULLEY
84	TORSIONAL DAMPER
85	CRANKSHAFT SPROCKET
86	ENGINE CRANKSHAFT
87	CRANKSHAFT UPPER BEARINGS
88	COOLANT PUMP GASKET
89	COOLANT PUMP
90	HEATER HOSE FITTING
91	ENGINE CAMSHAFT
92	COOLANT PUMP PULLEY
93	CAMSHAFT RETAINER
94	CAMSHAFT BEARINGS
95	FUEL PUMP OPENING COVER
96	OIL LEVEL INDICATOR TUBE
97	ENGINE CYLINDER BLOCK
98	INTAKE MANIFOLD OIL SPLASH GUARD
99	OIL LEVEL INDICATOR
100	CAMSHAFT SPROCKET
101	TIMING CHAIN
102	ENGINE FRONT COVER SEAL
103	ENGINE FRONT COVER GASKET
104	ENGINE FRONT COVER
105	CRANKCASE VENTILATION PIPE
106	CRANKCASE VENTILATION HOSE CONNECTOR
107	THROTTLE BODY INJECTION HEATER HOSE
108	THROTTLE BODY INJECTION COOLANT HOSE NIPPLE
109	EGR VALVE GASKET
110	FUEL INJECTION RAIL ASSEMBLY
111	EGR VALVE
112	THERMOSTAT
113	COOLANT OUTLET GASKET
114	COOLANT OUTLET
115	EGR VALVE VACUUM HARNESS
116	EGR CONTROLLER VALVE RELAY SOLENOID
117	ENGINE OIL LEVEL SENSOR

Index